Bible Talk

50 literal drawings explained

Bruce Benson

Heart Wish Books

Bible Talk:
50 literal drawings explained

Published by Heart Wish Books
Cambridge, Massachusetts

heartwishbooks@gmail.com

All Bible quotations are the author's
paraphrase unless marked

Scripture quotations marked (KJV)
are from the King James Version
in the public domain

Library of Congress Control Number: 2023912848

ISBN: 979-8-9867410-0-0

Nonfiction - Religion - Biblical Studies - Exegesis & Hermeneutics
Nonfiction - Religion - Christian Theology - General

Other books by Bruce Benson

AHA moments from the Bible

Jehovah's Witnesses Hate Jehovah

The Bible on Abortion: The shedding of innocent blood

Gay-affirming theology: An explicit exposé

The Catholic Church: femme fatale

Try my Bible Quiz

Speaking in tongues: Shamana bo-ho roe-toe

Joseph Reflects Jesus: Lifegivers

Otros libros del autor en español

Charla sobre la Biblia: 50 dibujos literales explicados

Momentos AJÁ de la Biblia

Los Testigos de Jehová odian a Jehová

La Biblia sobre el Aborto: El derramamiento de sangre inocente

Teología de la validación gay: Una exposición explícita

La Iglesia Católica: mujer fatal

¡Prueba mi cuestionario bíblico!

Hablar en lenguas: Shamana bo-jo ro-to

José refleja a Jesús: Dadores de vida

The inspired artist,

with the supernatural ability,

who did the drawings for this book,

is Katerina Rusakova

Contents

Welcome to my humble attempt to amuse and inform.

We'll be looking at Biblical sayings, and some of the false ideas most people have about God. I took poetic license. Angels don't have wings, God the Father and Jesus don't have long hair, and the devil doesn't have hooves, horns, or a tail. I portrayed them that way so you'd know who I'm talking about. No, I didn't do the drawings. They were done by an inspired artist according to my specifications.

I didn't do indexes. Look at it this way, I did you a favor. Now you get to take notes. I did my part. You can do yours. I do what I can, under the circumstances. Forgive me if any of the Bible references are wrong, or if there are spelling errors or typos. I create these books by myself, in a one-bedroom apartment, with no help-meet. These are homemade, self-published books. I'm Heart Wish Books. I do the writing, editing, design, and cover, and I decide how much white space there should be. I take great care to make the sentences look the way I want them, to make them more enjoyable for you to read. And I get attacked by the devil and his evil spirit-beings while I write my books. Yes, that's right, I don't have a degree from a seminary, or an ordination from a church. I'm just some nobody, someone you'd think was least likely to be doing this. I think people who know me figure someone else is writing these books and letting me put my name on them. You should know that about me. It might make you not want to read this book. Or, it could make you believe in God. He's proving to you that He exists. How else could a loser like me have created a book like this? And He can do the same for you. But, if you're a winner in this world, don't let it go to your head. God might chasten you, like He did to me, so I'd finally admit that He is my Lord and Savior. I thank Him every day that He keeps on showing me His love by chastening me, Hebrews 12:6.

This is my sixth book. This one is special. I can hardly sleep at night, I'm so excited about this book. I've decided that for the first time, I'm going to try to promote my books. I'm looking online for someone to help me. The star of this book is the drawings. Our Heavenly Father led me to an artist with a supernatural ability.

Bruce Benson

> One day, as Jesus was walking along the sea of Galilee,
> He saw two fishermen casting a net into the sea.
> They were brothers, Simon and Andrew.
> Jesus said to them, "Follow Me, and I'll
> turn you into fishermen who fish for people."
> They dropped their net and went with Jesus.
> Mark 1:16-18

"Fishing for people" means snatching souls out of hellfire, Jude 1:23. You get snatched if you have genuine faith, if you truly trust in Jesus, Ephesians 2:8. You get that faith by hearing a Christian teach the Bible, Romans 10:17. So, to be able to fish for people, Christians have to be students and teachers of the Bible.

> Go now, and teach everyone, everywhere.
> Tell them to obey the commandments I've given you,
> so they too can become My disciples.
> Jesus, Matthew 28:19-20

Christians fish for people by teaching them to obey the commandments Jesus gave us in the Bible. That's the work Christians are to be engaged in – not working at soup kitchens. Anyone can work at a soup kitchen. Christians are the only ones who can teach the Bible. Jesus wants fishers of souls, not do-gooders. Saving souls from hell by teaching them the Bible is the work Christians do – not protesting for rights, vegetable gardens, pot farms, concerts, bounce houses, or snow cones. You'll only attract fake Christians that way. Jesus doesn't want the people who go to a church for those things.

> If you fish for souls, you're wise.
> Proverbs 11:30

> If you lead many people to Jesus,
> you'll shine like the stars, forever, and ever.
> Daniel 12:3

> Jesus seeks and saves the lost.
> Luke 19:10

> The devil is your father.
> Jesus, John 8:44

If you think you're going to Heaven because you're a good person, then you're relying on your own goodness instead of the goodness of Jesus. But you're no better than a murderer.

> Cain murdered his brother.
> Cain is a child of the devil.
> 1 John 3:12

This is you,

> Whoever commits sin is a child of the devil.
> 1 John 3:8

You're not a good person. You're incapable of being good. You don't know what good is. You commit sin. We sin when we disobey God's laws, 1 John 3:4. To <u>commit</u> sin means you don't acknowledge your sins, you don't confess them to God, you don't repent of your sins (change your mind about them), and you don't want Jesus to cleanse you. You've made your heart hard because you love your sins. You're a child of the devil. But a child of the devil can become a child of God.

> If you make Jesus Christ your everything,
> and you commit yourself to Him, then He will
> give you the power and ability to become a child of God.
> John 1:12

And this will be you,

> God's children don't <u>commit</u> sin.
> 1 John 3:9

Then, when you pray to God, you'll say, "My Father," Romans 8:14-16, Galatians 4:6-7. God will welcome you to Heaven, because when He looks at you, He will see a good person, because you'll be clothed in the perfect goodness of Jesus, Psalms 149:4; Isaiah 61:10; Revelation 19:6-9.

Cast your bread upon the waters,
and you'll find it after many days.
Ecclesiastes 11:1

Revelation 17:15 says "the waters" are the people of every nation and every language. Jesus commands Christians to cast our bread upon all the people of the world. What is our bread?

I am the Bread of Life.
Jesus, John 6:48

I am the living bread
who came down from Heaven.
If anyone eats this bread
they will live forever.
The bread that I give is Myself,
which I will give to anyone
who wants to live forever.
Jesus, John 6:51

Christians cast our Bread upon the waters by feeding people the Word of God, the Food of Life, Jesus Christ, Jeremiah 15:16. Then, God's Holy Spirit can touch their heart, and they can repent, confess their sins to God, turn to Jesus as their Lord and Savior, and receive eternal life. And after many days, when we go to Heaven, we'll find the results of casting our bread upon the waters. We'll meet the people who were saved by hearing what we taught them from the Bible about Jesus.

The rain and snow come down from the sky,
and they don't return until they've
watered the earth to make it bud, and
produced seeds for the sower, and food for the eater.
And My Word that goes forth from My mouth is the same.
It will not return to Me empty,
but it will accomplish that which I please.
It will succeed in doing what I sent it to do.
God, Isaiah 55:10-11

That's Eve, talking to the devil in the Garden of Eden, in Genesis 3:1-7. But the King James Version (KJV) doesn't say it was the devil. It says Eve talked to a serpent.

Yes, but in Revelation 12:9, the KJV reveals the serpent to be, "that old serpent, called the Devil and Satan, which deceiveth the whole world." There was a time when the devil was good, very special, wise, and very beautiful, but he went bad, and he was in Eden, and God will kill him, Isaiah 14:12-20; Ezekiel 28:12-19.

The devil lies to your face while he wears a smile. And he gets you to believe his lies by claiming he's a Christian. You've never met anyone more intelligent, eloquent, charming, attractive, powerful, clever, sneaky – and deadly. The devil deceives people by disguising himself as "an angel of light," 2 Corinthians 11:14 (KJV). That means he pretends to be a messenger from God.

The devil is a liar and a murderer.
Jesus, John 8:44

God told Adam (and Eve) that they would die if they ate from the devil's tree, Genesis 2:17. But the devil put on a disguise. He told Eve that he was a tree-affirming theologian, and he convinced her that there was a good way to eat from his tree, Genesis 3:5. Eve ate, 2 Corinthians 11:3. And Adam ate, Genesis 3:6. Adam died, Genesis 5:5. Eve's death isn't recorded, but it's a given. Be warned – fake preachers are deadly.

The devil has a lot of fake preachers working for him, and he disguises them as angels of light – as smiling Christians, 2 Corinthians 11:13-15. They'll charm the pants off you. They, like their father, are deadly.

How can you spot the fakes? Give your life to Jesus, and study the Bible like your life depends on it, Acts 17:11. God will give you the ability to tell the true from the fake, Hebrews 5:11-14. Then you can warn people about the fakes, Ezekiel 3:18-21; Revelation 2:2,6.

HOLY
BIBLE

> Don't give your pearls to pigs.
> They'll crush them under their feet.
> Then they'll try to crush you too.
> Jesus, Matthew 7:6

The man in the drawing has some pearls. He knows they're beautiful. He's a good guy. He wants to share his pearls with others. So, he gave some to a pig. But the man was shocked. The pig didn't recognize the preciousness of his pearls. The pig crushed the pearls under his feet. And instead of showing gratitude to the man for sharing his pearls, the pig tried to crush him too.

In the Bible, pearls represent something very valuable. Each of the twelve gates in Heaven will be made from one pearl, Revelation 21:21. Jesus tells Christians how to get to Heaven. It's called the Good News. It's the most valuable pearl. And Jesus says this to all Christians,

> Tell everyone in the world
> about the Good News.
> Jesus, Mark 16:15

Jesus doesn't want us to share the pearls of the Good News with pigs. Did Jesus call people pigs? No. By comparing people's behavior to the behavior of pigs, Jesus painted a picture in our mind to help us see His point. When a woman says the man she dated was a pig, she means he acted like a pig. He didn't appreciate her. He was gross, vulgar, all hands. She's a person, with a mind, not just a body. So, she won't let him treat her that way anymore.

Jesus taught us by His example. When Jesus was brought before king Herod Antipas, the king asked Jesus many questions, but Jesus didn't answer any of them, Luke 23:8-9. King Herod Antipas is the one who murdered God's spokesman, John the Baptist, Matthew 14:1-13.

Jesus told us a story. There was a man who planted wheat in his field. But someone hated the man – and he went into the man's field, during the night, under the cover of darkness, while the man slept, and he planted poisonous weeds amongst the man's wheat. Later, when the man's workers saw the poisonous weeds growing together with the wheat, they asked the man if they should remove them. He said no, if you gather up the weeds now, you'll uproot the wheat. Let them grow together. And at harvest time, I'll tell the reapers to gather the weeds and burn them. Then you can gather the wheat and put it in my barn.

Matthew 13:24-30

The disciples asked Jesus to explain His story. Jesus said He is the Man who planted the wheat. And the field represents the world. The wheat is the children of His Kingdom. The one who hated Him, and who planted the poisonous weeds amongst His wheat, is the devil. The poisonous weeds are the children of the devil. The reapers are the angels. And just as weeds are burned in the fire at harvest time, so will it be at the end of the world. Jesus will send His angels to gather the children of the devil – all those who love the evil things that God hates, who won't stop doing those evil things, and who won't stop tricking others into doing them too. The angels will throw those evil people into a furnace of fire, where they will weep and wail loudly, and gnash their teeth, Matthew 13:36-42.

And what about the children of the Kingdom of God? Jesus said,

> Then the children of the Kingdom, the righteous ones,
> will shine forth like the sun, in the Kingdom of their Father.
> Matthew 13:43

Jesus concluded the explanation of His story by saying,

> Whoever has ears to hear, let them hear.
> Jesus, Matthew 13:43

The story is meant to have a sobering effect.

> Fishermen cast a net into the sea. And when the net is
> full of all kinds of fish, they pull it to shore. Then they
> sort out the good from the bad. They gather up all the
> good fish and put them in containers. Then they throw
> away all the bad fish. It's like the end of the world.
> That's when My angels will separate the evil people
> from the good. They'll throw the evil people into the
> furnace of fire, where there will be weeping,
> and gnashing of teeth.
>
> Jesus, Matthew 13:47-50

You might be thinking, Bruce, why are you talking about hell again? Because that's what Jesus did. In Matthew 13:40-42, Jesus said He will send people to hell (Yes, Jesus will). Then, just a few verses later, in Matthew 13:47-50, Jesus again said He will send people to hell. You can't talk about Jesus without talking about hell. You can't say you believe in Jesus if you don't believe there's a hell.

Jesus warned about hell, emphatically, and repeatedly, in direct commands, Matthew 5:29-30; 7:13,19; 10:28; Luke 13:3,5, and in stories, Matthew 22:8-13; 25:24-30,41. The day is coming, when Jesus will take the good people with Him to live forever in Heaven, and He will send the evil people to hell. People prance around like they own the place. They go on sinning like it's no big deal, as though God is a jolly bowl of jelly, who will say, "It's okay," forgive everybody, and open wide the gates to Heaven. No. God _is_ love, 1 John 4:8,16, but He's _not_ a fool.

> God is angry with the wicked every day.
> Psalms 7:11 (KJV)

Why is God angry about sin? Aren't you? What do you feel when you hear that someone murdered a child? Then why blame God for being angry? But sin isn't just murder. We're sinful by nature. We're rotten, inside and out. God's holiness and sense of justice is 100% pure, and beyond our ability to fully comprehend. It's so serious, that God had to be crucified to save believers from our sin, Matthew 26:62-68; 27:27-37. Every one of us is infected with the sin that Adam brought into the world, Romans 5:12. We sin when we break God's law, 1 John 3:4.

The Bible says this about Jesus,

> He was received up into heaven,
> and sat on the right hand of God.
> Mark 16:19 (KJV)

God came to earth to live as a man called Jesus, so He could die on a Roman cross, Psalms 22:16; John 3:14. Jesus rose from death after three days, Matthew 12:40; Revelation 1:18; 5:6-14. He stayed for forty days, Acts 1:3. Then, Jesus the Man went back to Heaven, Acts 1:9-10.

> This Man, after He had offered
> one sacrifice for sins for ever,
> sat down on the right hand of God.
> Hebrews 10:12 (KJV)

God is Spirit, John 4:24. But the Bible often uses a figure of speech that brings God down to our level, and speaks of Him as though He has some of the physical features and feelings that we have. The Bible says God has hands. God's "right hand" is the power and abilities He has because He is God. Exodus 15:6,12; Psalms 32:4; 77:10-11; 118:15-16; 139:10; Isaiah 48:13

The verse we started with at the top of the page, Mark 16:19, shows us Jesus the Man. And it also shows us that Jesus is God. Jesus sits on the right hand of God. The word "on" was translated into English from the Greek word *ek*. It means "out from." It means Jesus came from God. Didn't we come from God too? Yes, we did, Ecclesiastes 12:7. But it's different with Jesus. The Bible teaches us that Jesus <u>is</u> God. John 1:1-3,14,18; Colossians 2:9

What is Jesus the Man doing while He's sitting on (at) God's right hand? He's still acting on behalf of believers. He's talking to God about us. Jesus is making sure that we make it to Heaven. And, Jesus the Man is sitting at God's right hand waiting for God to turn those who made themselves His enemies, into the place where He rests His feet (that's a figure of speech). Psalms 110:1; Romans 8:34

What will God do with you if you reject the salvation made available by the sacrificial death of the Lord Jesus Christ? Will He punish you by subjecting you to torture that never ends? Will He keep you alive, awake, and aware forever, so you'll experience every second of agony? No. The God of the Bible won't do that. And I'm very suspicious of anyone who says He will. I wouldn't want them for a roommate. They're projecting their own sadistic desires on God. The Bible says God will consume the wicked. He will end their existence.

But some verses seem to clearly say that God will sentence unbelievers to eternal conscious torment (ECT). So, we need to know the absolute literal truth about the fate of unrepentant sinners. That truth will be our Guide. When we encounter verses that seem to teach ECT, we'll face them with confidence, because our Guide will be with us. We begin the search for our Guide with the Bible's most famous verse,

> If you truly believe in the sacrificial death of Jesus,
> then you will not perish – you'll live forever, with Jesus.
> John 3:16

Believers live forever. Unbelievers perish. The word "perish" is # 622 in the Strong's Concordance. It's the Greek word *apollumi*. You can also use # 622 to study *apollumi* in books by others, like Zodhiates, and Kittle. To find it in Kittle, you look up # 622 in the New Englishman's Greek-English Concordance and Lexicon, by George Wigram. It gives you a number, 1:394. That means you go to Kittle, volume 1, page 394. In our verse, John 3:16, the word "perish" means to "destroy." It refers to unbelievers, those who will not live forever. Their soul will die in hell. If you look up # 622 in the New Englishman's Greek-English Concordance & Lexicon by George Wigram, you'll see every place where it's used in the New Testament. It says in Matthew 2:13 that king Herod wanted to "destroy" (# 622) Jesus. Herod wanted to kill Jesus. Some say # 622 can't be used to teach that God will end people's existence in hell by killing their soul. Why? Because # 622 is used for the death of the physical body, and when a person's physical body dies, they don't go out of existence because their soul is still alive.

(Continued on page 28)

No. What they're missing is that the Bible sometimes says things according to our point of view. For instance, Ecclesiastes 1:5 says the sun rises and sets. But we know the sun stands still. It's the earth that rises and sets around the sun. The Bible says the sun rises and sets because that's how it appears to us. And when a person dies, it appears to us that they cease to exist, because they never come back, forever.

Let's continue the search for our Guide,

> Those who can kill your body are unable
> to kill your soul. So, don't fear them.
> Instead, fear Him who is able to destroy
> both your body and soul in hell.
> Jesus, Matthew 10:28

Jesus said the "body and soul" of the wicked will meet the same fate. Both will be "destroyed" (# 622) in hell. The soul of the wicked will die. The Bible calls that the "second death," Revelation 2:11; 20:6,14; 21:8. The first death is the death of the physical body. What's left after that is the soul. The second death is the death of the soul. It's what God does to you if you refuse to clothe yourself in the righteousness of Christ. Jesus said He will kill those who go to hell, not torture them forever. When the soul dies, it's over.

But Jesus said hell is "everlasting punishment." Yes, in Matthew 25:46, Jesus said the doomed will go to "everlasting punishment," and Christians will go to "eternal life." Jesus used the same Greek word for the "everlasting" punishment of the doomed that He used for the "eternal" life of Christians. Because of that, some argue that if you say the everlasting punishment of the doomed in hell isn't really everlasting, then you can't say the eternal life of Christians in Heaven is really eternal. Are they right? No. You need to know how the word "everlasting" is used in the Bible. But first, I have to tell you that the King James Version (KJV) uses the word "hell" as the name for three different places. You can find them in the Strong's Concordance by looking up the word "hell." (I'll tell you how to do that on page 48). When Jesus spoke of hell, the word He used is Gehenna, Matthew 5:29. That's the actual hell, the final destination of the wicked.

There's also Hades, Luke 16:23, which is called "hell" in the KJV, but is just a temporary place for people who've died. And, in 2 Peter 2:4, in the KJV, we read that God threw some bad angels into "hell." But that's not hell. It's a place called Tartarus. It's a prison where God is holding those bad angels until Judgment Day.

After Judgment Day, those bad angels will be moved from Tartarus to Gehenna, to be consumed, Matthew 25:41. They'll no longer exist. Jude 1:6 says the angels in Tartarus are held in "everlasting chains." But their stay in Tartarus is temporary. Everlasting chains for a temporary punishment. So, it's the chains that are everlasting, not the punishment. "Everlasting" means the chains are indestructible.

In Matthew 25:41, when Jesus said He will tell the doomed to go into "everlasting" fire in hell, He used the same Greek word for "everlasting" that Jude used for "eternal" in Jude 1:7, where Jude said Sodom and Gomorrah suffered the vengeance of "eternal" fire. But those cities were destroyed, God killed every person in those cities. So, how could the people of Sodom and Gomorrah be suffering the vengeance of "eternal" fire now? They're not. "Eternal" fire means the fire that killed them was eternal, or indestructible – not the punishment. And if you go to hell, you'll be consumed by indestructible fire. God is that fire.

Romans 6:23 (KJV) says, "The wages of sin is death; but the gift of God is eternal life through Jesus Christ our Lord." In that verse, eternal spiritual life is the opposite of spiritual death. The righteous go to life that's everlasting in the sense that the life will never end. The wicked go to death. You can't die forever. Death is a one-time occurrence. You die and it's over. The wicked go to punishment that is everlasting in the sense that their punishment, the death of their soul, is irreversible.

What about Revelation 14:11? It says the smoke from hell will rise up forever. Well, our Guide wants us to look at Isaiah 34:9-10. There, God is talking about how He will destroy the wicked nations, so that "the dust will become brimstone, and the land will become burning pitch." God said, "It will not be quenched night or day, and the smoke from it will go up forever." God is talking about nations here on earth. He said the smoke of their destruction will go up forever. But that's impossible.

It's impossible because the Bible says this earth will be burned up and there will be a new earth, 2 Peter 3:10-13; Revelation 21:1. Okay, but what about Revelation 20:10? It says the devil will be thrown into hell and be tormented day and night forever.

Our Guide wants us to learn about the fate of the devil by looking at Ezekiel 28:11-19. God is talking to "the king of Tyrus" there, but He's really talking to the devil. Verse 13 says, "You were in Eden." In verse 18, God tells the devil that He will bring forth a fire from his midst that will devour him. God tells the devil that He will bring him to ashes upon the earth. Logic says God can't both burn up the devil into ashes and torment the devil forever.

The best way to study the New Testament is by looking to the Old Testament. In Genesis 49:26, Jacob referred to "the everlasting hills." Hills aren't everlasting. They'll be destroyed when Jesus renews the earth. The Bible is not stating literal facts when it says the smoke from hell will rise up forever, or that the devil will be tormented forever, or that those in hell go into everlasting punishment. That's figurative, poetic language – emphatic declarations used to express the eternal finality of the destruction of the body and soul of the wicked in hell.

Malachi 4:1 tells us about Judgment Day. It says, "the day is coming that will burn like an oven, when all the proud, and yes, all who do wickedly – will be stubble." It says, "the Lord of Heaven's armies has declared that the day that's coming will burn up the wicked, so that it will leave them neither root nor branch." And Malachi 4:2-3 says, "the righteous people will tread down the wicked people, and the wicked people will be ashes under the soles of the righteous people's feet."

In Matthew 13:30 and 40, the burning up of the wicked is compared to the burning up of poisonous weeds pulled up from a wheat field. And it says in Matthew 3:12 that Jesus (yes, Jesus) will "burn up" the wicked in hell. The words "burn up" are # 2618. It means to burn something to ashes, burn it up completely, utterly consume it.

The apostle Paul went to the city of Ephesus, and God did miraculous things through Paul in the name of Jesus.

A lot of the people there had been practicing evil magical arts. But as an act of repentance many of the people who believed in Jesus, publicly burned the books they had been using for those evil arts, Acts 19:11-19. The Greek word used to say they "burned up" those books is # 2618. It's the same word used in Matthew 3:12 to say that Jesus will "burn up" the wicked in hell. The books about evil magical arts went out of existence when they were burned up. And evil people's souls will go out of existence when they're burned up in hell.

Deuteronomy 4:24 says God is a consuming fire. Isaiah 1:28 says God will consume the wicked, and Psalms 37:20 says, "into smoke they will consume away." In John 15:6, Jesus said the wicked will be thrown into the fire and burned. Deuteronomy 29:20 says God will blot out the names of the wicked. It means He will blot <u>them</u> out. God will not blot out Christians, Revelation 3:5. Our Guide is showing us that God will not torture the wicked forever, but will consume them. They will be utterly destroyed, never to be seen or heard from again, forever.

There's a few other things to consider. First, what purpose would God have in torturing people forever? What end would it serve? Would it teach them a lesson? No. There's no point in that, their fate is sealed. Would it teach others a lesson? No. The others are incapable of doing wrong and are eternally safe in Heaven. Secondly, who is the God of the Bible? Yes, God is our Lawmaker and Judge, Isaiah 33:22. He is the Disciplinarian, Hebrews 12:6. God feels anger every day because of evildoers, Psalms 7:11. And He will pass sentence on the unrepentant. But what satisfaction would He get from torturing people eternally? Those who say God will do that don't know Him. God is not a sadist.

Thirdly, how could believers enjoy Heaven if we know that God is torturing people in hell? Our former family and friends are screaming in pain, and we're supposed to ignore that and enjoy the pleasures of Heaven? No. That's not possible. And it's not what will happen. After Judgment Day, when all the believers are safely in Heaven, that's when God will wipe away all the tears from our eyes. There will be no more death, no more sorrow or crying, and no more pain, because all those things will have passed away, Revelation 21:4.

Popular culture and bad church teachings have given the world images of hell as a place where God watches people scream and writhe in pain while He tortures them with fire. No. The fire of hell is not the fire we know. It's not the fire that burns your hand when you touch it. The fire of hell is a spiritual fire. It's the fire of God. When God appeared to Moses in a fire in a bush, Moses was amazed because the bush was unharmed by that fire, Exodus 3:2-3.

Jesus baptizes believers with that fire, Matthew 3:11. And Jesus will burn up the wicked in hell with that same fire, Matthew 3:12. God's fire can warm your heart, or consume you in hell. If you're sent to hell, you'll weep, and gnash your teeth. But it won't be because you're burning in literal fire (you won't be). It will be because of the intense remorse you'll be feeling, now that you've finally faced the reality that you wasted your life loving the world, instead of loving God.

Hell is necessary. God has to protect His children. He can't have unrepentant sinners in Heaven. They'll just cause trouble. They'll ruin it for everybody. That's the problem we have here on earth, evil people, stupid people. It won't be like that in Heaven. God will protect those who love Him. So, God has to keep out the stupid people. He has to end their existence. Eternal torture? No. There's no reason to do that. God isn't a sicko. He doesn't get pleasure from torturing people.

The unsaved will all be done away with and forgotten. It will be like they never existed. Yes, it is sad. But they were so stubborn. Salvation was available, but they refused to receive it.

People often ask, "Why does God allow evil?" I tell them that's the wrong question, and the right question is, "Lord, will you have mercy on me, a sinner?" So why isn't that my answer to the question, "Will God subject the wicked to eternal conscious torment?" Because I gave the same answer to "Why does God allow evil?" that God gave. It's in the Book of Job, chapters 38-42. I gave the answer that the Bible gives. My answer to the question, "Will God torture people forever in hell?" is the same answer that the Bible gives. The answer is, "No, the Bible doesn't teach that."

> I'll remove your heart of stone,
> and give you a new, soft heart.
> God, Ezekiel 36:26

It's bad. Your heart is hard. It can't be repaired. You need a transplant. Only one surgeon can do the operation – God, the Great Physician, Mark 2:16-17. Your heart is evil by nature, Mark 7:20-23. You hate to obey God's law. You get stiffnecked, and harden your heart toward God, Deuteronomy 9:6. And He really hates that, Zechariah 7:11-12.

Genesis 6:5; Jeremiah 17:9

God wants to give you a new heart. It comes loaded with new software. It gives you the desire and ability to obey God. Jesus talked about it, John 3:5. God doesn't want anyone in Heaven who didn't get the new heart. That's understandable. Why would God want to live with people who love evil? Would you?   Psalm 51:10; 2 Corinthians 3:3

A very big price had to be paid in order to make this new heart available. All of us disobey God's law (that's sin, 1 John 3:4). What happens when you break the law? You get punished. So, before you get the new heart, do you have to be punished for your sins? No. Why not? Because someone already took the punishment. Who? God Himself. God let Himself be born into a human body like ours. He lived a perfectly sinless life. But He was executed on false charges, Matthew 26:57-68; 27:28-37. Then He rose from death, Matthew 28:5-8. We call Him Jesus, which means, God our Savior, Matthew 1:21. Why did God do that for us? Because He loves us, John 3:16; 1 John 4:8,16. The punishment for sin is death in hell. Jesus saves believers from hell. But we still suffer illness and the death of our flesh bodies as a result of sin.

Why doesn't God just give everybody the new heart? Because you can't force people to love you. That's not true love. God only gives the new heart to people who reverence Him, and who want to love Him by obeying Him, Matthew 13:18-23; John 14:15-24. Okay, so how do you get this new heart? Take the first step of obedience. Fall on your knees before God with a desire to obey Him, and ask Him to save you, Matthew 4:17. Admit to Him in a childlike way, your utter sinfulness, hopelessness and helplessness, Luke 18:10-14.

> If you haven't been born again,
> then you can't go to Heaven.
> Jesus, John 3:3

Jesus said that to a man named Nicodemus. And Nicodemus asked, "How can an old man like me enter a second time into my mother's womb to be born again?" John 3:4. The word Nicodemus used for "old" is the Greek word *geron*. It's # 1088 in the Strong's Concordance. It's where we get the English word "geriatric," referring to elderly people.

Jesus responded to Nicodemus' question by repeating His original statement a little differently. Jesus said, "You can't go to Heaven if you haven't been born by water and Spirit," John 3:5. By "water" Jesus does not mean water baptism. Being dipped in water has no effect on a person. Water baptism is a symbolic act which represents a believer's dying with Jesus and rising again to live a new life, Romans 6:1-23. Baptism is only for those who've already been born again. Cornelius was baptized after he was born again, Acts 10:44-48.

In John 7:37-39, Jesus used water to represent God's Holy Spirit. In His response to Nicodemus, Jesus called God's Holy Spirit "water," and "Spirit." Jesus used a figure of speech. He gave the same meaning to two different words, making His statement stronger, to make us think.

Being born again means you're regenerated because God makes His home in your heart – literally. Everything changes. You can't "enjoy" sin like you used to. You might try to, but it won't work. You might fall into your old sins, but you won't stay there. God's Holy Spirit living in you will get you out of those sins, put you back in your right mind, and get you back to doing the work God is giving you to do, Proverbs 24:16; Luke 22:32. You belong to God now. He will make sure that you're constantly changing for the better. God will cleanse you of sin, Ephesians 5:26; Titus 3:5; 1 John 1:7-9, discipline and chasten you, Hebrews 12:6, comfort you, John 14:1,15-19,23-28, and He will never leave you, Hebrews 13:5. God's Holy Spirit living in you is God's promise to you that you're going to Heaven. You have His guarantee, John 6:37, 39-40; 10:27-30; Ephesians 1:12-14. Nothing can ever change that, Romans 8:9,28-35.

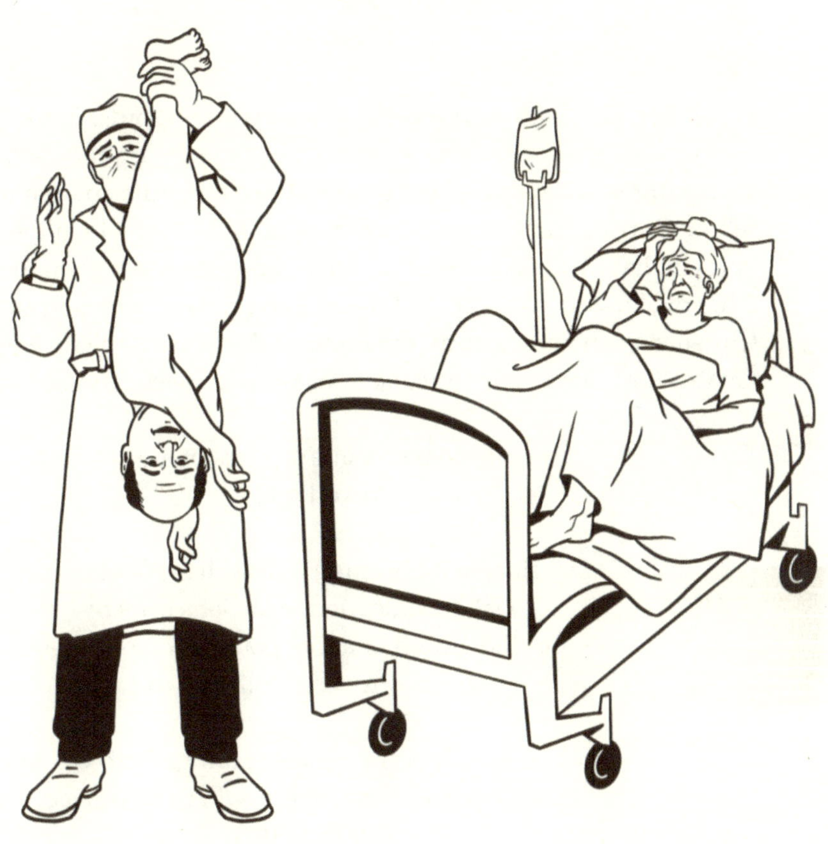

You need violent winds to propel a sailboat.
So, it's amazing that you can steer
that sailboat wherever you want,
just by moving a little rudder.
And your little tongue is like that rudder.
You can use your tongue to steer your boat
wherever you want it to go.
James 3:4-5

When the Bible says your tongue, it means your words. Control your words, and you'll steer your spiritual health in the right direction. If you're immersed in Bible study, and you're fortunate enough to find a fellow Christian who is also immersed in Bible study, then the two of you will have conversations that are filled with words from the Bible. Oh, how blessed you'll be. But if you hang around with so-called Christians, who don't study the Bible, and who resist being engaged in God's Word, then your conversations will be useless and harmful.

A wholesome tongue is a tree of life.
Proverbs 15:4

A sincere Bible student uses their tongue
to speak the knowledge of God correctly.
But the mouth of a fool pours out foolishness.
Proverbs 15:2

The mouth of the obedient brings forth wisdom.
But the fraudulent tongue will be destroyed.
Proverbs 10:31

Lord, stand guard at the door of my lips,
and keep watch over my mouth.
Psalms 141:3

My Father and Me are one.
Jesus, John 10:30

"Jesus, The Son of God," is a role played by God. When God came to earth to live as a man named Jesus, He did the things that a man does, which means He prayed to God. God was on earth praying, and God was in Heaven hearing His prayers. God the Son prayed to, and obeyed, God the Father. But Jesus _is_ God the Father. Don't believe me? Then look at this,

A Child will be born, a Son will be given ...
and He will be called Wonderful, Counselor,
The Mighty God, The Everlasting Father,
The Prince of Peace.
Isaiah 9:6

That Child was born around six hundred years after Isaiah 9:6 was written. The announcement of His birth says, "Today, in Bethlehem, the Savior was born. He is Christ the Lord," Luke 2:11. When Jesus was born, they called Him Emmanuel, which means "God with us."
Matthew 1:23

Someone said they refuse to believe in a God who would send His Son to die. No. God didn't pick up His flip phone and call Jesus, and say, "Son, I need You to do Me a favor – go to earth and be born as a man and let people nail You to a cross." No. God Himself came to die for the sins of believers. God died on that cross. That was God's blood that was shed when Roman soldiers crucified Jesus. That Son was God Himself. I'm tired of hearing pastors say, "Jesus is equal to God." It's misleading and confusing. Jesus isn't equal to God. Jesus _is_ God.

But Jesus said He was sent by His Father. Yes, but when Jesus said that, He was speaking as the Son of God, Jesus the man, God the man. It was God who sent, and God who was sent. God can be in more than one place at the same time. This is an instance where $1 + 1 = 1$.

1 + 1 = 1

I keep hearing Christian pastors say things like, "God in three persons," and "the three members of the trinity." They call Jesus, "the second member," and God's Holy Spirit, "the third member." They sound like Mormons. The Bible never uses those expressions.

"The Church of Jesus Christ of Latter-day Saints," aka, "the Mormons," has an official website called, churchofjesuschrist.org. On that site, under "Godhead," in an article called, *The Trinity of traditional Christianity is referred to as the Godhead*, they say, " ... while some believe the three members of the Trinity are of one substance, Latter-day Saints believe they are three physically separate beings ... " And about God the Father, they say, " ... Latter-day Saints believe He has a human-like body but is immortal and perfected ... " And here's what they say about Jesus, " ... He, like His Father, has a physical body ... "

No. The Father, Son, and Holy Spirit are not three separate people. They're one person. There's one God. The religions of the world always make counterfeit copies of the one true God. That's why they have a trinity of three persons, three gods. Worshiping gods will send you to hell. You're breaking the First Commandment, where God said,

> Get your gods out of My face.
> Exodus 20:3

No, I'm not a modalist. Modalists say Jesus and God's Holy Spirit don't exist eternally. I'm not saying that. God came to earth to speak to us, to tell us the way to Heaven. That's why Jesus is called the Word of God. Jesus is <u>not</u> the eternal <u>Son</u> of God. He is the eternal <u>Word</u> of God, John 1:1. Jesus is not a separate person from God. He is God's words in a human body. Your words are not a separate person from you. After Jesus rose from death, He told believers He would ascend to Heaven in His physical body, and then He would come to us again. Speaking as the Son of God, Jesus said He and the Father will make their home in our heart. He's talking about the Comforter, God's eternal Holy Spirit.

> John 14:15-17,23; 15:26; 16:7

> I will not leave you comfortless: I will come to you.
> Jesus, John 14:18 KJV

MEMBERS ONLY

If the blind lead the blind,
they'll both fall into the pit.
Jesus, Matthew 15:14

The pit is hell. The blind leaders are those who say they're teachers sent by God, but God didn't send them. The blind they're leading are people who don't want the truth, so they let themselves be led astray by liars.

In 2 Thessalonians 2:9-12, God said if you refuse to receive a love of the truth, that He freely offers, then He will let the devil give you a strong delusion. You'll believe the devil's lies. You'll be damned because you refused to take pleasure in righteousness.   Matthew 13:15-17

The devil has churches. They're called Christian churches. The devil has priests, ministers, reverends, and bishops, who call themselves Christian teachers and leaders. They're smart and sneaky. They give you lies. They call their lies truth, and they call truth lies, Isaiah 5:20. They choose blindness. And if you choose to close your eyes too, then they'll take your hand and lead you to the pit.

For the leaders of this People cause them to err;
and they that are led of them are destroyed.
Isaiah 9:16 (KJV)

Beloved, don't believe everyone who says they teach the Bible.
Test their teachings to see if they really are from God's Word,
because there are many false teachers all over the world.
1 John 4:1

As time goes on, those who deceive themselves and deceive others
will be constantly inventing increasingly evil teachings and practices.
2 Timothy 3:13

How do you know the true from the fake? Compare what they teach with what the Bible teaches, just like the Bereans did in Acts 17:11. Hebrews 5:11-14 says God gives discernment to Christians who exercise and train our mind in the Bible, with constant, diligent study. Then we're able to tell good from evil, and the true from the fake.

THE PIT

If you want to find out how God feels about abortion, then start by studying the words used in Psalms 139:13-17. You need a KJV Bible, which I used in this study. And you need a Strong's Concordance, and books like the Brown-Driver-Briggs Hebrew and English Lexicon.

Verses 13 and 15 say, "Thou hast covered me in my mother's womb," and, I was, "curiously wrought." Look at those words in the original Hebrew. They say God knits together the child's body in the womb. Verse 14 says a child in the womb is, "fearfully and wonderfully made." The technological wonder of the creation of a human body in the womb proves there's a Creator. We're awestruck by God's greatness. The human body is incredibly complex. God's creation of the child's body in the womb is skillful, exquisite, wonderful, unfathomable, awesome, and beautiful. The child in the womb is God's masterpiece. Verse 13 says, "Thou hast possessed my reins." The word "reins" means your innermost self, your thoughts and feelings, the person you are. The word "possessed" means to own. It's used in Genesis 14:19 to say that God is the creator and owner of the earth and sky. It means a baby in the womb is God's property. God creates that baby, and He owns that baby. It's wrong to say you have a right to take the life of that child. There is no such right. That means there is no such thing as a woman's right to abortion. Abortion is the murder of a child, God's child.

How can it be that children are being killed in the womb, in the shelter that God provided for their protection? There's only one way people would accept that. They're being deceived. The murder of a child is called "women's health care," and "reproductive rights." Some people say they're Christians and they tell the lie that Jesus is for abortion. Those so-called Christians never tell you that abortion ends the life of a precious little person, whose body was being weaved together by God. That person is alive. They suck their thumb. Abortion makes that little person bleed, feel pain, and die, just like any person who's murdered.

> Don't murder a person.
> God, Exodus 20:13

> I'm not here to do away with Exodus 20:13.
> Jesus, Matthew 5:17

> Why havn't you read Genesis 1:27?
> It says that right from the beginning,
> God has been making people male and female.
> And Genesis 2:24 says that's why a man will
> leave his father and mother and cleave to his wife.
> Jesus, Matthew 19:4-5

Do you have a Strong's Concordance? If you're serious about studying the Bible, then you must. And you need a King James Version Bible, because the Strong's uses the words from that version. Take your Strong's and look up the word "cleave" that Jesus used in Matthew 19:5, at the top of this page. You'll see a list of all the verses where "cleave" appears. Find our verse, Matthew 19:5. Now look all the way to the right. You'll see a number. It's 4347. Look up that number in the Greek dictionary (not the Hebrew) in the back of the Strong's. You'll see that "cleave" is made up of two words. One of them is number 2853, which means "glue." And the other is number 4314, which means "to." Jesus said a husband and wife are to be glued to each other (see drawing).

If the pastor of your church tells you you're not capable of looking up words in the languages that the Bible was originally written, then I have a question for you – why are you letting them tell you what to do? If you're a Christian, God's Holy Spirit tells you what to do.

The Bible is clear that God created only two genders – male and female, and only one sexual orientation – heterosexuality. And God created only one marriage, and it's only for a man and a woman. People hate it that I say, "the Bible is clear." But it is. If you can say the Bible is unclear about homosexuality, which, in the Bible is such a serious matter, a matter of eternal life and eternal death, then you can say the Bible is unclear about how a person goes to Heaven, or whether Jesus is God, or whether He died and resurrected, and all the other things that are a matter of eternal life and eternal death.

God said He will send you to hell if you don't repent of your homosexuality. And He did not say it in a way that can't be understood. He said it in a way that's impossible to misunderstand. Don't let anyone deceive you, including yourself.

> Jesus told a man, "Follow Me."
> But the man said, "Lord, first
> let me go and bury my father."
> And Jesus said, "Let the dead
> bury the dead."
> Luke 9:59-60

The New Testament was written in Greek. The Greek word used here for "dead," is *nekros*. It's where we get the English word necromancer, meaning someone who claims to be able to communicate with the dead (they can't). Jesus said, "Let the nekros bury the nekros." How can dead people bury dead people? That's impossible. So, the ones being buried are cadavers, stiffs. And the ones doing the burying are alive (they'd have to be) but they're dead in some other way.

Sin and death entered the world through the sin Adam committed in Genesis 3:6. It says in Romans 6:23 that "the wages of sin is death" (KJV). The way God sees it, Adam was our representative, Romans 5:12. We go through life spiritually dead because of Adam's sin, and because of our own sins. Before we became Christians, we were alive physically, but dead spiritually. We were "dead in sins," Ephesians 2:5.

When we became Christians, we, in a manner of speaking, died, when Jesus died, and we were buried with Jesus, Romans 6:4. When Jesus rose from death, we rose with Him as a new person. The old person that we were, who was dead in sins, dead spiritually – they died. And, the new person we became is not *nekros*, not dead, but alive, spiritually.

> Now that you're one with Christ,
> it means the person you were has died.
> And you've become a brand-new creation,
> different from what you were before.
> Are you getting this? Everything is new!
> 2 Corinthians 5:17

52

Who will free me from this body of death?
The apostle Paul, Romans 7:24

The "body of death" Paul wants to be freed from is his physical body. Paul wants out. He's discovered that the hunk of flesh he lives in is a big problem. When Paul became a Christian, he became a completely new person, Romans 6:18; 2 Corinthians 5:17; Galatians 5:22-24.

A Christian's new person has a newfound hatred of sin. We make every effort to avoid it. And, our new person is <u>not</u> going to hell because of our sin, like our old person was, Romans 8:1. Why do Christians change like that? Because Jesus does it. He does it to those who believe in Him. How? By living in us, Ephesians 4:20-24. Paul said, "I was crucified (died) with Christ, but I live. But it's not me. It's Christ living in me," Galatians 2:20. All of this was made possible because Jesus gave Himself for us, died on a cross for us, 1 Thessalonians 5:9.

But we still have this body of death strapped to us. It's a body of death because it's a body of sin, and sin is the reason for death. Our physical body, including our mind, still has all our old sinful urges embedded in them. And our physical body is harassing our new person. So, there's a struggle going on between the Christian's new person and our sinful physical body. Paul describes that struggle in Romans 7:14-25. He's describing what everyone who becomes a Christian experiences. The great apostle Paul had the same struggle that every Christian has.

That struggle is a mark of a genuine Christian. Nonbelievers and fake Christians do not experience that struggle.

Paul wants to be freed from sin, as every Christian does. Who will free us? Jesus will. That will happen at the death of a Christian's physical body. Then Jesus will free us from sin and death. We'll never sin again. We'll live forever with Jesus in Heaven, in a new, sinless, spiritual body.

Romans 6:23; 7:24-25
1 Corinthians 15:42-45,50-58

HOLY
BIBLE

A man said to Jesus, "Lord, I will follow You,
but first let me go and say goodbye to my family."
And Jesus said to him, "You'll never get to Heaven
if you look back while you're plowing your way there."
Luke 9:61-62

If your feelings for your mother and father
are stronger than your love for Me, it means
you don't have what it takes to be in My army.
And if your feelings for your son or daughter
are stronger than your love for Me,
then you don't really love Me.
Jesus, Matthew 10:37

Following Jesus is everything, Luke 9:23; 14:27. Nothing in this world is more important, Luke 5:27-28. No person or thing should keep you from following Jesus, 2 Timothy 2:3-4. Our love for Jesus should be more intense than our love for are spouse, parents, siblings, and children, and more intense than our love of ourself, Luke 14:26.

If your mother and father tell you they'll disown you if you become a Christian, you become a Christian anyway. Jesus doesn't want you to work for Him if your heart is somewhere else. If you look back after you join Jesus, you're not a true disciple, you don't really believe, Genesis 19:26; Luke 17:32. Working for Jesus is serious business. It's about people's souls. It's the difference between eternal life and eternal death. If you look back, then you'll go off course, and you'll be more likely to teach error and commit sin. Here's the right response,

Two brothers, fishermen,
named James and John, were in a ship,
mending nets with their father, Zebedee.
Suddenly, Jesus appeared.
Jesus said to James and John, "Follow Me."
They didn't say a word.
They immediately got off the ship,
left their father, and followed Jesus.
Matthew 4:21-22

Jesus went to a well to find a certain woman. He knew she understood the value of water. Jesus asked her to give Him a drink of water. But before she could draw the water, Jesus said if she knew about the free gift that God gives, and if she knew who He was, then she would ask Him for a drink of water, and He would give her Everspringing Water. Jesus said if you satisfy your thirst by drinking water from the well, you'll become parched again. But, Jesus said, you'll never be dry if you drink the water He gives, because it will be a well in your heart, a fountain springing up from within you, giving you eternal life.

John 4:1-14

Then Jesus told her He knew she was living in sin. She admitted that He was right. Why is that important? The Everspringing Water is a free gift given by God. But He only gives that gift to people who thirst for it, who know they are sinners, who hate their sin, and want to be freed from the guilt of sin.

A person walks through a desert dying of thirst. Then they find water and live. Water is life. Sinners walk through this world dying from sin. Then we find the Everspringing Water, and we find life – eternal life, and refreshment. We find relief from the guilt of our sin. One water is physical and the other is spiritual. The Everspringing Water is the Holy Spirit of Jesus.

John 4:16-19

When Jesus said you will never thirst again, He was assuring us that once He gives us the Everspringing Water, once He saves us, He will keep us saved, forever, John 6:37, 39-40; 10:27-30; Romans 8:28-39. God's fountain of water springing up in your heart will give you new feelings – the feelings God feels. You'll truly know God. You'll follow Jesus by living your life the way He lived His, John 13:15; 1 Peter 2:21.

> With joy you will draw water
> out of the wells of salvation.
> Isaiah 12:3

What harmony is there
between Jesus and the devil?
2 Corinthians 6:15

That's a statement in the form of a question. The answer is obvious.
There is no harmony between Jesus and the devil. In the original Greek,
it doesn't say "the devil." It says "Belial." That's a derisive nickname for
the devil. It comes from a Hebrew word that means "wickedness."

There are people who are called the children of Belial. When Jezebel
needed men to give false testimony against an innocent man in a death
penalty case, she got two sons of Belial to do it, 1 Kings 21:1-19. You
can read how Jezebel died and what happened to her body in 2 Kings
9:30-37. Who are the children of Belial? That would be you. Oh no, you
say, you're not doing anything as bad as giving false testimony in a
death penalty case. But you are. You're staying silent about people's
deadly sins and not warning them. God sees things in black and white.
You're either a child of God, or a child of the devil, 1 John 3:9-10; 5:19.
But you can switch sides. Humble yourself before God, and tell Him
you want Jesus to save you, Matthew 4:17; John 3:16; Acts 16:29-31.

The word "harmony" in that verse is the Greek word *sumphonesis*,
which means "one sound." It's related to the word "symphony," a group
of musicians who are all in agreement. This is a warning to Christians.
Jesus is the Holy One. The devil is the evil one. The devil is the father
of evil, John 8:44. The children of Jesus must never sing harmony with
the children of the devil. It means we don't mix their beliefs with ours.

Psalms 101:1-8; 1 Corinthians 10:20-21;
2 Corinthians 6:14; 1 Timothy 5:22

That doesn't mean we hide indoors, Matthew 10:16; John 17:15-18.
We're to be among people and have a dutiful love for them, for the
same reason Jesus did – to get them to change their mind about sin,
Mark 2:15-17. We don't condone their evil beliefs by staying silent, as if
everything's okay, 2 John 1:10-11. We warn them. God said if we don't
warn them, then He will ask us why we didn't care that they were
headed for death in hell, Ezekiel 3:18-1.

Acts 20:26-27;
1 Corinthians 5:9-10; Ephesians 5:11-12; 2 Timothy 2:24-26

Don't play a trumpet when you
perform an act of compassion.
Jesus, Matthew 6:2

There was a man who had been unable to walk since birth, Acts 3:2, and he was over forty years old, Acts 4:22. Every day, people carried him to the gate of the temple, so he could ask passersby for a donation. One day, the apostles Peter and John were on their way into the temple, and the man asked them for some money. Peter said, "I don't have any money. But I'll give you what I do have – In the name of Jesus Christ the Nazarene, get up and walk," Acts 3:3-6. A Nazarene is someone who is from, or who lives, in the town of Nazareth.

Then Peter took hold of the man's right hand and lifted him up. The man jumped up and walked, and he walked into the temple with Peter and John, walking, and jumping, and praising God. All the people who saw what happened, ran to Peter and John, filled with wonder and amazement. But Peter said, "Stop gawking at us as though we're some sort of gods. You don't actually think it was us who made that man walk, as if we have the ability to do that, or because we're such good people, do you?" Peter knew it was God who healed the man. He gave God all the glory. He didn't toot his own horn, Acts 3:7-12. There's a reason why God used Peter to heal the man. It says in Hebrews 2:3-4 that God used miracles as a way to let the people know that someone was speaking for Him, and not an impostor. So, Peter gave a sermon. He taught them that Jesus is God, and that Jesus gave His life as a sacrifice for the sins of anyone who will believe in Him. Peter told the people to repent, and believe in Jesus.   Acts 3:13-26

When people play a trumpet while they're doing good, they're drawing attention to themselves. Some churches are full of trumpet players. They adorn themselves in overly-pious evening gowns and accessories. And they call themselves high holy this, and right reverend that. They love the honor and praise of the people. Jesus calls them hypocrites. He means they're playacting. They don't have real love and compassion. The so-called good things they do are phony. They don't know God and He doesn't know them. On Judgment Day, Jesus will tell them to go away, Matthew 7:21-23

A Christian friend brightens a Christian's face,
like an iron file sharpens an iron ax head.
Proverbs 27:17

I've been going on Christian dating sites. I'm lonely. God said it's bad
for a man to be alone (my paraphrase), and I agree, Genesis 2:18. I need
female companionship to cheer me up. I want a good woman to talk to,
Proverbs 5:15-19; 18:22; 19:14; 31:10-12,30; Ecclesiastes 4:9-12; 9:9.

But the Christian dating sites are the same as most Christian churches.
They're full of people who just call themselves Christians. A lot of the
women on the Christian dating sites have a long list of their activities.
There's volleyball, kayaking, board games, painting, skiing, badminton,
goodminton, and soooo many pickleball players. And I wonder – when
do they have time to study the Bible? It's very rare to find one who says
she studies the Bible, or who even mentions the Bible. They're looking
for a husband. But how could they think a marriage would work if
they don't study the Bible? A humble Christian woman who studies the
Bible is the most beautiful sight in the world. But I think I have a better
chance of seeing Big Foot.

When a Christian shares knowledge, truth, and wisdom from the Bible
with a fellow Christian, we are their best friend. We enliven their spirit,
strengthen their heart, give them encouragement, enrich their mind,
build them up. We feed them their spiritual food, their daily Bread, the
Bread of Life, and we inspire them to action. We sharpen them like iron
sharpens iron. And it shows in their face. We see the joy, comfort,
contentment, and happiness that comes from hearing the Word of God
from a fellow Christian. But most Christians in churches don't know
that. They haven't truly tasted the Word of God. They're not being
taught that they need to know the Bible so they can teach the Bible.
There's a lot of bad pastors, ego cases, who keep their people enslaved
to them, like babies sucking their mother's breasts. They never let the
babies grow up. They make them think they're not worthy to study the
Bible on their own. Most people in churches are terrified at the thought
of having an interpretation that's different from their pastor's. They
think that's the unpardonable sin. Most churches churn out lots of
useless so-called Christians. Don't follow that crowd. Be sharp.

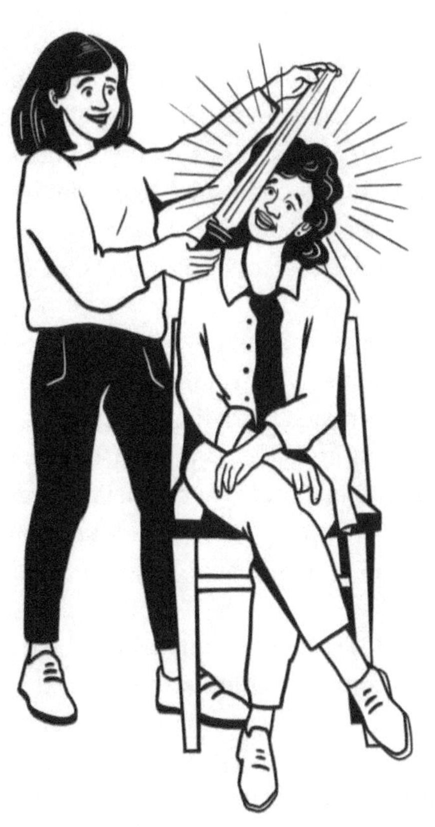

Above all, take up the Shield of the Christian Faith,
to snuff out all of the devil's flaming arrows.
Ephesians 6:16

Jesus is the Christian's Shield. God told Abraham, "I am your Shield," Genesis 15:1; Romans 4:20.

What are the devil's flaming arrows? It doesn't say in that verse. But we can see what the devil does by looking through the Bible. The devil convinced Eve to eat from the tree that God said not to eat from, Genesis 2:17; 3:1-6; the devil provoked king David to number his troops in a sinful way, 1 Chronicles 21:1-8; the devil entered Judas just before Judas betrayed Jesus; Luke 22:1-6; and the devil filled the heart of Ananias to lie to God's Holy Spirit, Acts 5:1-6.

The devil is a crafty, malicious, powerful supernatural being. The Bible calls him, "the accuser," Revelation 12:10. The devil wants Christians to sin, and he knows each Christian's weakness, Matthew 16:21-23. And he has an army of invisible, evil spirit-beings fighting with him against Christians, Ephesians 6:12. We can never let down our guard. The devil is too powerful an enemy. This is serious business. The devil wanted to sift the apostle Peter like wheat, Luke 22:31-32.

Christians must never get comfortable. The devil can catch us sleeping. The devil uses traps, schemes, and sneak attacks. And he will attack us through people, even the ones closest to us, Matthew 16:21-23. Christians have to be constantly on the lookout, wearing the armor, Ephesians 6:11, always thinking, watching, praying, Ephesians 6:18. Christians are soldiers. We have to be engaged in warfare against sin and the devil's deception, every day. 1 Timothy 1:18; 6:12; 2 Timothy 4:7

But the Christian's victory is assured. Jesus promised, Romans 8:1-39. He defeated the devil and his soldiers, Hebrews 2:14; Colossians 2:15. Christians resist sin for holiness' sake, and to show the glory of God. We have to do our part. But we don't fight the devil. Jesus fights the devil for us. We pray, "Deliver us from the evil one," Matthew 6:13.
2 Corinthians 10:3-5; 2 Timothy 4:18; 1 Peter 3:22

> When people tell you they're speaking for Me,
> examine them carefully, because hungry wolves
> are wearing sheep's clothing.
> Jesus, Matthew 7:15

A lot of the fake Bible teachers wear a costume. They do that to make you think they're speaking for God. Or maybe they're trying to hide their phoniness. Real Bible teachers don't wear a costume. Jesus didn't. Judas had to point Him out to His captors, Matthew 26:47-50.

In Matthew 7:15, Jesus is saying don't assume people are genuine because they wear a holy hat, or because they have a PhD from a Bible school, or call themselves priest, pastor, bishop, or reverend. Don't assume they must be speaking truth because they wear a clerical collar and a pretty stole, or smile warmly, speak eloquently, and praise God.

> Observe and avoid the Bible teachers
> who love to walk around in long robes.
> Jesus, Mark 12:38

Do you know what wolves do to sheep? That's why Jesus gave this warning. Jesus said there are wolves pretending to be Bible teachers. But even if a pastor or Bible teacher is not a wolf in sheep's clothing, don't assume that everything they say is correct. And never let a pastor tell you what to do. It's not their place to tell you what to do, or what to believe. Never obey a pastor. Yes, Hebrews 13:17, in the King James Version, seems to say obey <u>them</u>. But that's not what it means. It means learn from them, and follow their example – if what they teach and do is from the Word of God, the Bible, 1 Peter 5:2-3. Your pastor is there to serve you by feeding you the Word of God, John 21:15-17; Acts 20:28. <u>Obey the Word of God</u>, Luke 8:21; 11:28; John 15:23. You don't have a relationship with Jesus through a pastor, church, or denomination. Your relationship is not with your pastor. Your relationship is with Jesus Christ, through your own personal Bible study. If you're a Christian, you have to interpret the Bible yourself. Jesus will teach you through His Holy Spirit, John 14:18,26; 16:13; 1 John 2:27. How do you get the ability to know who are the wolves? God gives it to Christians whose minds are always in the Bible, Hebrews 5:11-14.

Is there a brawling wife in your house?
Then you're better off living in a corner of the roof.
Proverbs 21:9

Marriage is great. It's wonderful. And of course it would be, because God created it. It's so good to have someone, and to be cared about and loved. But a brawling wife ruins it. She's impossible. And as much as it's going to hurt to be apart from her, as much as you love her, as much as you'll miss her, as much as it hurts to be alone, you have to separate. You've got to do it for your spiritual health, for the good of your Christian walk. You have to love God more than you love her.

Love Me more than you love your wife.
Jesus, Luke 14:26

What about a woman who's married to a fool? Abigail was. But Abigail was a good woman. She didn't follow her husband. She acted wisely. And God blessed her for it. God killed her fool husband. Then Abigail married a good man.   1 Samuel 25:1-42

God wants a Christian wife to submit to her husband, like a private submits to a sergeant in the army, Ephesians 5:22-24. That's pleasing in God's eyes. Their ministry will run smoothly and effectively that way.

What about the husband? God said the love a Christian husband shows his wife is to be the same love Jesus showed to His wife, the Church. Jesus showed His love for His wife by sacrificing Himself, giving Himself over to crucifixion for her. Jesus wants a Christian husband to love his wife with that same self-sacrificing love.   Ephesians 5:24-25,33

What was Jesus' father's name? Did you say Joseph? When Jesus was twelve years old, He went to Jerusalem with His parents, Mary and Joseph, to celebrate the seven-day festival of Passover (Exodus 12:1-51). When it ended, Mary and Joseph started their journey back home to Nazareth. Jesus wasn't with them but they assumed He was in the caravan with their friends and family. After they'd been on the road for a day and hadn't seen Jesus, they looked for Him in the caravan but they couldn't find Him, Luke 2:40-45. So, they went back to Jerusalem. And, after three days of searching, they found Him. They were amazed to see that Jesus was sitting in the temple, and all the Bible teachers were sitting in a circle around Him, listening to Him speak, and asking Him questions. The Bible teachers were astonished at the answers Jesus gave to their questions, and the understanding He had, Luke 2:45-47.

When Mary found Jesus, she said. "My Child, why have You treated us this way? Pay attention! You sent Your father and me into a panic. We looked everywhere for You." Then we hear the very first words of Jesus that are recorded in the Bible. Jesus reminded Mary who His Father is. He said, "Why were you looking for Me? Didn't you know that I have to do what My Father told Me to do?"   Luke 2:46-52

Whenever Jesus said, "My Father," He meant God, Matthew 7:21; 16:17; 18:10; 20:23; 24:36; 26:53. And, when Jesus prayed, He always called God, "Father," Matthew 16:17; John 17:1,5,11,21,24,25; 20:17. Jesus did what His Father, God, told Him to do. Just before Jesus died on the cross, He said, "It is completed," John 19:30. And, after three days and nights, Jesus rose from death, Matthew 12:40; 1 Corinthians 15:1-4, as the Old Testament said He would, Psalms 16:10 (the apostle Peter said that verse is about Jesus, Acts 2:22-28); Psalms 22:12-22; Isaiah 53:10-12.

Yes, you were right in one way if you said Joseph was Jesus' father's name. Joseph was the legal guardian of Jesus when Jesus was a child. But Joseph had nothing to do with the conception of Jesus in Mary's womb. Jesus was conceived in Mary's womb when God's Holy Spirit enveloped her. Mary was a virgin when she gave birth to Jesus.
                    Isaiah 7:14; Matthew 1:18; Luke 1:34-35

HAPPY
FATHER'S
DAY
FROM YOUR SON,
JESUS

> People don't turn on a lamp
> and then cover it with a basket.
> They put it in a place where it can
> give light to everyone in the house.
> Jesus, Matthew 5:15

> I am the light of the world.
> Whoever follows Me
> will not walk in darkness.
> They will have the Light of Life.
> Jesus, John 8:12

Jesus says this to Christians,

> You are the light of the world.
> Now go and shine at people.
> Jesus, Matthew 5:14,16

Jesus makes Christians into light, His light. And He sends us to shine His light to the world. The man in the drawing is doing something insane. If Christians cover up our light, it's not only insane, it's cruel. People are walking in darkness to a spiritual death. Only the light of Jesus gives life – eternal life. Some people hate Christians because we shine at them by speaking the truth from the Bible. If that hatred makes a Christian hide their light under a basket, then they're being disloyal, derelict, and cowardly.

Jesus tells Christians,

> Be very happy when people chase after you like dogs to try
> and ruin you. Be very happy when they spew hateful words
> at you, and tell lies about you – all because you belong to Me.
> Rejoice! And I say, be exceedingly glad, because you're reward
> in Heaven will be great.
> Jesus, Matthew 5:11-12

God sends lazy people to the ant,

> Go to the ant, sluggard.
> Listen carefully to what she says.
> She'll teach you how to be wise.
> Proverbs 6:6

God speaks highly of ants,

> Ants don't need supervisors,
> drill sergeants, life coaches, or a
> mighty government to motivate them.
> Ants are the wisest of the wise.
> On their own initiative they
> spend the hot days of summer
> cultivating their food. And then,
> in the cool days of autumn,
> they gather up their harvest.
> Proverbs 6:7-8; 30:24-25

And God has a warning for lazy people,

> How long will you sleep, sluggard?
> When will you wake up?
> What did you say, sluggard?
> You need a little more sleep?
> A little more slumber?
> A little more folding of the hands?
> Oh sluggard, you'll only gather up poverty.
> Proverbs 6:9-11

The poverty of the sluggard is a poverty of wisdom. It's a poverty of the knowledge and understanding that God gives only to those who seek Him with ant-like determination and fortitude.

Who's in a state of bliss?
It's the person who watches and
waits at Wisdom's gates, day after day,
sleepless, like a soldier on guard duty,
treasuring up and protecting her words.
It's the person whose mind is focused on Wisdom,
who hungers for her, and obeys her every word.
Proverbs 8:34

Wisdom is better than jewels.
And all the things that people desire
cannot be compared to her.
Proverbs 8:11

Receive my instruction instead of silver,
and knowledge rather than gold.
I love those who love me.
And those who seek me early will find me.
Wisdom, Proverbs 8:10,17

If you find Wisdom, you find life,
and you receive favor from the Lord.
Proverbs 8:35

Stupid people's willful ignorance will slay them,
and the prosperity of fools will destroy them.
Proverbs 1:32

If you hate me, you love death.
Wisdom, Proverbs 8:36

People listened to Jesus, the Wisdom of God, Luke 19:47-48; 21:38.
Wisdom said the same thing that Jesus said, Luke 11:49; Matthew 23:34.

All the treasures of wisdom and
knowledge are stored up in Jesus.
Colossians 2:3

WISDOM

> Do you think I'm here to bring peace?
> Wrong. I'm not here to bring peace. I'm here to
> thrust a sword between a son and his father,
> and between a daughter and her mother, and
> a daughter-in-law and her mother-in-law.
> Jesus, Matthew 10:34-35

In Leviticus 26:6, God told the children of Israel that if they obey His laws, then the sword will not go through their land. In that verse, the word "sword" means "war," just like it does in Jeremiah 43:10-11. If they obey God, they will have peace, and no wars.

Isaiah 9:6 says Jesus is called "the Prince of Peace." And when Jesus was born, the multitudes in Heaven said, "Glory to God in the highest, and on earth, peace, and kindness toward humankind," Luke 2:14. Okay. Then why did Jesus say He will thrust a sword of war between Christians and members of our biological family? People hated Jesus because He spoke truth from the Bible – just as it is. When you become a follower of Jesus, you too will speak truth from the Bible – just as it is. And people in your family will react violently, Mark 13:12-13. They'll hate you because you follow Jesus. That's why Jesus said He's thrusting a sword of war between you and members of your family (the ones members who reject His offer of peace and kindness), Proverbs 9:8; 29:27; Galatians 4:16.

Why did Jesus say it that way, that He didn't come to bring peace, but war? He did it to get our attention, startle us, get His message through our thick skull, and force us to use our mind by studying the Bible, thinking hard, and meditating on His words to unravel His riddle. That's good for us, Romans 12:2; Ephesians 5:26.

> The world hates Me. So, they'll hate you too.
> If you were of the world, they'd love you as one of their own.
> But they'll hate you because I called you out of the world.
> When they do all kinds of evil things to you, remember,
> they treat you that way because you belong to Me, and
> because they don't know the One who sent Me.
> Jesus, John 15:18,19,21

> You scribes and Pharisees devour widow's houses,
> while you pretend to be deep in prayer to Me
> (all I'm hearing you say is "Blah, blah, blah").
> You're a bunch of hypocrites. You're doomed!
> Jesus, Matthew 23:14

Beware of fluent parasites on TV, who try to bedevil you with their urgent warnings to send your firstfruit seed money <u>now!!</u> They say this window of blessings will only be open for a short time, and if there's any delay, you'll miss out on having your illness healed, or getting that new job (as if God will run out of blessings). Send $50 and receive a napkin anointed with crumbs wiped from Pastor Pooterpopper's beard! No! Never! You don't need their healing oil, communion cups, or prayer shawls. One genius finds dates on the calendar, like 1/23/45, and says you have to send him money on that date so God can bless you. No! God won't reward you with material blessings because you sent money to crooks. They're frauds, hucksters, greedy people, who make cruel, fake promises. They prey on your discontent, your desire to be rich. They take advantage of people who have illnesses. And they do it in the name of Jesus. They prod elderly people on pensions to scrape together $1000 and send it to them. They say they need it to spread the Gospel. But they get very wealthy and live in luxury by coming up with scam after scam to devour widow's houses.

What should you do? Have your own relationship with God by studying the Bible with books, and praying to God, yourself, at home. Don't look to someone else to bring you God's blessings. If you're sick, don't worry about whether God heals you or not. Are you poor? Good. Let it humble you. It says in Proverbs 15:16 that it's better to have just enough, with reverence for God, than it is to have many possessions without peace of mind. Don't wish you had more. Don't wish you could have what other people have. Always thank God for what you do have. A real genius is the person who figures out how to make the most of what God gives them. They use it to share the Bible with people and teach them the Gospel of Jesus Christ, the only Way a person can go to Heaven. A real genius has knowledge and wisdom from God, peace of mind, contentment, joy, and salvation – the real riches.

Our eyes have a mind of their own. They crave pleasure, both good and bad. Sin enters through the eyes. Eve decided to eat from the devil's tree, after she looked at it and saw that it was delightful, Genesis 3:6; The "sons of God" (angels, Job 1:6) saw how beautiful the earth women were, so they left Heaven to seduce them, Genesis 6:2; David, the king of Israel, seduced another man's wife after he saw her bathing. Then he murdered her husband, 2 Samuel 11:1-27 (But David confessed his sins, 2 Samuel 12:13; Psalms 51:1-19, and God forgave him, 2 Samuel 12:14). God said in Proverbs 4:25-27, that it's our responsibility to control our eyes. God wants Christians to make every effort to keep all the parts of our body away from evil. But we're teeming with filthy urges. So, God helps us. He lives in the heart of a believer, takes up residence there. And He gives us a new nature.

> When you live your life
> according to the new nature
> that I've given you, then you
> won't give in to sinful urges.
> God, Galatians 5:16

> When you feel sin turning you
> to the right and to the left,
> I'll whisper over your shoulder,
> and I'll say, "Walk this way."
> God, Isaiah 30:21

> I am the Way, the Truth, and the Life.
> Jesus, John 14:6

Christians are in constant hand-to-hand warfare with our sinful urges. It's a knock-down, drag-out fight. There are losses and gains. But we make steady progress toward victory because we walk "this way." Jesus is the Way. His Holy Spirit and His Word strengthen us, assure us, comfort us, and keep us going, Ephesians 3:16-17. God wants us to enjoy the eyes He gave us by keeping them locked forward, looking straight ahead, intently fixed on Him, not turning to look at sin.

Joshua 1:7-9; Psalms 1:1-6; 25:15; 119:37; Proverbs 16:17

Your Word is a lamp to my feet,
and a light to my path.
Psalms 119:105

I am the light of the world.
Whoever follows Me
will not walk in darkness,
but will have the light of life.
Jesus, John 8:12

Christians walk in the light. It means we walk in obedience to what God said in the Bible. It means we follow Jesus, who lived as a man and obeyed God perfectly, Hebrews 5:8-9. When you walk in the light you show the evidence that you're sincere, that you're going to Heaven because you're a genuine follower of Jesus. To walk in darkness means you love sin, and you refuse to turn to God to save you from sin.

God is angry with those who love their sin, who love darkness. He calls them the children of disobedience, Ephesians 5:6-8. Christians are not to do what they do. We used to walk in darkness, 1 Corinthians 6:11. But Jesus gave us His light, and we're to live our lives as children of light. We walk in the light by keeping our mind in the Bible. That's what David did. He prayed to God, "I'm filling my mind with Your Word, because I don't want to sin against You," Psalms 119:11.

In Deuteronomy 6:6-7, God commands believers to treasure up His Word in our heart, to teach His Word to our children, to meditate on His Word when we're sitting in our house, walking down the street, going to bed at night, and waking up in the morning. We sincerely do our best to obey God, obey His law. God rewards us by giving us the ability to obey Him, Romans 8:1-16; 1 John 1:5-7.

Sincere people are happy, because we obey God's law.
Psalms 119:1

Let the path of the wicked be dark and slippery.
Psalms 35:6

HOLY
BIBLE

The god of this world has blinded the mind of those who
don't believe, so they're unable to see the light of the glorious
Good News of salvation made available through Jesus Christ.
2 Corinthians 4:4

Your "god" is whatever you love instead of God. Some make
themselves their god, Philippians 3:19. God created the world perfect,
Isaiah 45:18. Then we filled the world with sin, Romans 5:12. The devil
is the god of the sin of the world. Sin is an ace up the devil's sleeve,
Hebrews 2:14. If you love and serve sin, then the devil is your father,
John 8:44, and he's your god, Ephesians 2:1-3. Does the devil blind
unbelievers? Look at this,

They're not able to believe in God, because, as Isaiah 6:9-10 says,
<u>God</u> blinded their eyes and hardened their heart, so they can't
see with their eyes, and can't understand with their heart, and
can't change their mind about sin. So, God can't save them.
John 12:39-40

Do you have to worry that God might not like you, and that just
because He doesn't like you, He might blind you to the truth and make
you not believe, and then send you to hell because you don't believe?
In Exodus 4:21, God said to Moses, "I will harden Pharaoh's heart."
Second Thessalonians 2:11 says, "God will send people a powerful
fraud, and they will believe that a lie is the truth." Jeremiah 4:10 says,
"Oh no! Lord God, I can't believe it. You used deceptive methods to
lead the people astray."

Jesus told a very important story about someone He called the Sower.
He told it twice. The first time, Jesus told the story to a great multitude
of people while His disciples were also there listening. But the second
time, Jesus told the story only to His disciples, after the multitude of
people had gone home. And this time, when He told the disciples the
story in private, Jesus didn't tell it to them as a story. Instead, Jesus
spoke to them plainly. He explained to them who and what the people
and things in the story represented.   Matthew 13:1-23

(Continued on page 88)

The disciples asked Jesus why He spoke to the people in stories.

And Jesus said,

> Because it's been given to you to know how to
> go to Heaven, but to them it is not given.
> Jesus, Matthew 13:11

Is Jesus unfair? Did God blind unbelievers? I'll tell you, but first, look at what God told the prophet Isaiah to do to people. God told Isaiah to,

> Harden their heart, and make their ears stupid, and shut
> their eyes, or else they might see with their eyes and hear
> with their ears, and understand with their heart, and turn
> from their sin in repentance and receive salvation.
> Isaiah 6:10

Why is God telling Isaiah to shut people's eyes so they won't see the truth and be saved from hell? Is God prejudiced? Does God force some people to sin and go to hell?

Suppose when you're a child, you tell your mother that you want to jump off the roof of the house. And she says, "Well, go ahead then and break your leg if you want to." If you took her literally then you'd jump. But you have to look deeper. She's really saying, "You'll break your leg if you jump off the roof – so don't do it!" God is being sarcastic. He's saying, "Ignore Me then, if you want to, and go ahead and die in hell." But God doesn't want anyone to die in hell, 2 Peter 3:9.

Isaiah speaks for God. It's God who's saying He will harden their heart. This is an instance where someone, God, is said to be making people do something but it's really the people who are doing it. God isn't hardening their heart. He's letting the people harden their own heart. Yes, that's an odd way of saying it, to say God is doing it when He isn't. It's a Hebrew idiom. The word idiom comes from the Greek word *idios*. In Luke 9:10, we read that Jesus met "privately" with His apostles, away from the crowds. The word that's translated "privately" in that verse is that same Greek word, *idios*.

An idiom is a way of saying something that's only used by one group of people. It's their own private way of saying things. Every group of people uses idioms. People from outside their group might have no idea what they mean. The word "idiot" also comes from the Greek word *idios*. That's because if you think for yourself, you'll be called stupid by mediocre minds.

The Bible uses Hebrew idioms in both the Old and the New Testament. So, in Jeremiah 4:10, when Jeremiah said God used deceptive methods to lead the people astray, what he meant is that God <u>let</u> the rebellious people be led astray by the deceptive methods used by false teachers. And, in Exodus 4:21, when God said He will harden Pharaoh's heart, He meant He will let Pharaoh harden his own heart.

God had a good reason why He let Pharaoh be the ruler of Egypt and why He let Pharaoh harden his own heart (Yes, God decides who will rule the nations of this world, Daniel 4:32; Romans 13:1). Pharaoh was holding the children of Israel, God's people, in slavery. God sent Moses to Pharaoh with the message, "Let My people go," Exodus 5:1. But Pharaoh hardened his heart and wouldn't let the children of Israel go. So, God worked miracles that were witnessed by Pharaoh, and by Pharaoh's people, the Egyptians. The Egyptians worshiped animals. God did the miracles to show the Egyptians that He is God.

So, you could say God hardened Pharaoh's heart in the sense that He let Pharaoh harden his own heart. That's because Pharaoh's hard heart worked into God's plan. But, only one person is responsible for the hardening of Pharaoh's heart, and that is Pharaoh himself, Exodus 9:27,34; 10:16-17. God said this to Pharaoh,

> Haven't you wondered why I made you the Pharaoh,
> the king of Egypt, and why I let you live, even though
> you've hardened your heart and disobeyed Me over and
> over? It's because I used your rebellion and stubbornness
> as an opportunity to show My power, so that people in all
> the world would know that I am the one true God, the God
> who lives, unlike the dead idols that people worship.
> God, Exodus 9:16-17

When two Israelite spies went to spy out the land of Jericho, God led them to a good woman named Rahab. She told them they'd heard that God did the miracle of drying up the Red Sea so the children of Israel could escape from Pharaoh and his army, and how, after the children of Israel passed through the sea, Pharaoh's army tried to pass through too, but God closed up the sea again and killed Pharaoh's army.

Exodus 14:21-31

Rahab said that when she heard what the God of the Israelites did, she was in awe of God's greatness, and she knew that He is the only God. God saved Rahab, and He put her in the genealogy of Jesus.

Joshua 2:9-11; Matthew 1:5

How did God harden Pharaoh's heart? By not killing Pharaoh. God showed mercy to Pharaoh, just like He shows mercy to all of us by not killing us, not executing us for our sins. Will you thank Him for that and turn to Him in repentance, or will you harden your heart and use His mercy as an opportunity to keep sinning? Will you blind yourself to God's mercy? Will you find false teachers who'll whisper in your ears that your sins are not actually sins? Those false teachers work for the devil. They'll happily tighten the blindfold around your eyes.

Isaiah 6:9-10 is quoted in five of the Books of the New Testament (Matthew 13:14-15, Mark 4:12, Luke 8:10, John 12:40, and Acts 28:26-27). In Matthew 13:14-15, it says, "the people closed their eyes, so they could not see, and not hear and understand, and not repent, and not go to Heaven." Unbelievers let the devil blindfold them.

Zechariah 7:11-12

If you're not convinced by my idiom argument, look at Luke 11:1-4. The disciples asked Jesus to teach them how to pray. Everyone knows that one of the things Jesus taught them to pray is, "Lead us not into temptation." Jesus tells His disciples that we should ask God to not lead us into temptation to sin. Jesus is using a Hebrew idiom. What Jesus means is, ask God to <u>not let you</u> be led into temptation to sin – ask God to make a way of escape, 1 Corinthians 10:13. Can I prove that? Yes. It says in James 1:13 that God never sins, and, it says God never leads anyone into temptation to sin. The devil tempts believers. God tests us.

Okay Bruce, got it. You're saying it means, "Don't let us be led into sin." Are you saying then that God can stop someone from sinning? Yes, that's what I'm saying. Can you prove it? Yes, I can. In Genesis 20:1-18, Abraham and his wife Sarah went to a city called Gerar.

Sarah was a beautiful woman, Genesis 12:11. And Abraham was afraid that if the men of Gerar knew Sarah was his wife, then they might kill him and take her. So, Abraham told people she was his sister. Then the king of Gerar, king Abimelech, took Sarah, thinking she was single.

But God came to king Abimelech in a dream at night, and said to him, "Hey! You're a dead man. The woman you've taken is a man's wife." But at that point Abimelech hadn't gone to bed with Sarah, he hadn't touched her. And he explained to God that Abraham, and even Sarah herself, told him that she was Abraham's sister. God said He knows all about that. And God told Abimelech that He kept him from sinning against Him, that He kept him from touching Sarah, Genesis 20:6.

So, God kept king Abimelech from sinning. But God didn't keep the Pharaoh of Egypt from sinning. No, He didn't. But that doesn't mean you can say it was God's fault that you sinned because He didn't keep you from sinning. It says in James 1:14 that when you're tempted to sin, it's because you've been enticed and drawn into sin by your own lust.

Your sin is 100% your responsibility.

So, when God said He hardened Pharaoh's heart, and He blinded people to the truth, and when Jesus said He speaks to the people in parables so they won't receive the truth that will save them – they're using Hebrew idioms, just like when Jesus tells His disciples to ask God not to lead us into temptation to sin.

God hardens a person's heart by telling them the truth. He knows it makes them harden their heart. He doesn't want people to harden their heart. But He has to tell them the truth about sin and salvation. If He didn't tell them, then He would be unjust. God can't judge people without first telling them the truth. But God does not harden anyone's heart and force them to sin and go to hell.

Then what about Jacob and Esau? Romans 9:11-13 says, "God loved Jacob, and hated Esau – before they were born, before they did any good or evil thing." Yes, and it also says God loved Jacob, and hated Esau, "so that His purpose would stand, according to election, not because of works (in this world), but because of God who calls."

Why did Jesus go to people like Peter, Andrew, James, John, and Levi, and call them simply by saying, "Follow Me?" Did Jesus show mercy on them, and call them to follow Him for no reason?

Matthew 4:18-22; Mark 2:14

No. Jesus did that because He knew them before they did any good or evil thing in this world. Jesus knew them from before. Why did they drop their fishing nets, leave their father, and follow Jesus? Because they were elect. The elect followed Jesus before we were born. It says in Ecclesiastes 12:7 that when you die, "the dust returns to the earth, and the soul returns to God." If we return to God, then we came from God.

Some don't like that. They think Jesus was unfair to choose Peter and the other elect the way He did, and leave the others to choose whether or not they will be saved. But it's because those who aren't elect didn't do what the elect did before they were born. That's why God explained in Romans 9:14-16 that He is not unfair, that He shows mercy and compassion on those He wants to – because they're elect, as He explained to us in Romans 9:11.

Can a person choose to be saved? Of course. The Bible says some choose not to be saved, Matthew 13:15. If you can choose not to be saved, then you can choose to be saved. John 1:11-12 says some people choose to receive Jesus, and some choose not to receive Him.

It's absurd to say God had no reason to hate Esau before Esau was born. God doesn't hate someone for no reason. That's what crazy people do. It's because of the evil that Esau did before he was born that God hated him. If you say there was nothing Esau did to make God hate him, then you're accusing God of being an unjust judge. Only an unjust judge hates someone for no reason.

God is not unjust. God loves good people who do good, Psalms 145:20; John 14:21, and He hates evil people who do evil, Psalms 5:5; 11:5. When you say God hated Esau for no reason, you're saying God broke His own law. Here's what God said in His law,

> Do not sentence an innocent person to death.
> God, Exodus 23:7

If you say Esau didn't do anything to make God hate him, then you're saying God hated an innocent man, and sentenced an innocent man to death in hell. How could Esau be innocent? Because he hadn't been born yet when God hated him. He hadn't been tainted with the original sin of Adam. So, if you say Esau didn't do anything before he was born to make God hate him, then you're saying Esau was innocent.

God had to have hated Esau before he was born because of evil things Esau did before he was born. It can't be any other way, or else God is evil, and that would contradict everything the Bible teaches about God.
> Romans 5:12;
> 1 Corinthians 15:22

And God didn't create some people who will go to Heaven, and other people who will go to hell – no matter what, as some teach. People who teach that are slandering God. They don't know God. They're calling Him evil, like He's some sort of heartless monster in a cruel sci-fi novel.

No, God gives everyone a chance to be saved. God is not a respecter of persons (faces). The apostle Peter said God welcomes anyone from any nation if they want to love and obey Him, Acts 10:34-35. Peter said God taught him not to call any person unworthy of salvation, Acts 10:28.

God doesn't reject you because you're not pretty, or because you have a low IQ, or because of the color of your skin. God is just, fair, and impartial. He goes by your heart, 1 Samuel 16:7.

> Does God deal with people unjustly? No way! Never!
> Romans 9:14

The most famous verse in the Bible, John 3:16, says "whosoever will."
That means anyone can be saved by Jesus if they want to. But people
don't want the light of Jesus to shine on them because they want to hide
in the darkness to do their sins. They perish because they refuse to
receive God's gift of a love of the truth, 2 Thessalonians 2:10.

> People love the darkness instead
> of the light because they're doing evil.
> Jesus, John 3:19

But as long as there is breath in you, there's hope. At any time you can
turn to God for forgiveness and salvation. It doesn't matter what you've
done, no matter how evil, how many times, or for however long. God is
good, loving, merciful, and compassionate. He wants you to turn to
Him. There's nothing you could have done that would make God reject
you, if you come to Him sincerely – absolutely nothing.

God would receive Esau, king Saul, the Pharisees, Judas Iscariot,
murderous dictators, rapists, child molesters, liars, and adulterers, if
they turn to Him in sincerity. He's even willing to accept you and me.
He only accepts the humble and contrite ones. Don't delay. Do it today.
The fool repents tomorrow.

> The Lord draws near to you when you feel
> crushed and brokenhearted over your sinfulness.
> Psalms 34:18

In Leviticus 11:1-23, God said, "Don't eat rats, etc." But now, most churches, pastors, and Bible translations are doing much harm to people's health by making the outrageous claim that Jesus did away with what God said in Leviticus 11:1-23, and that Jesus said Christians can eat catfish, pigs, lobster, leeches, snakes, dogs, cats, bats, and rats.

When they make that outrageous claim, they're adding their own ideas to something Jesus said when He was dealing with some fake religious leaders, called Pharisees. The Pharisees were oppressing the people by making them do a bogus hand-washing ritual. They told them they had to do the ritual before they ate so they wouldn't take in sin with their food. Jesus scolded the Pharisees for lying to the people. Then Jesus said something to the people. This is the saying that people are adding their own ideas to. Jesus said, "It's not what goes in your mouth that defiles you," Matthew 15:11; Mark 7:18.

But He didn't say that to do away with Leviticus 11:1-23. His saying has nothing to do with <u>what</u> you eat. The people already knew that God said don't eat rats. That wasn't the issue. Jesus said it to assure them that they wouldn't be taking in sin if they ate without first doing the Pharisees' fake, man-made ritual. Jesus told them where sin comes from. It comes from your mind, Matthew 15:18-19; Mark 7:20-23. And, Jesus interpreted His saying for us by giving the context of His saying. He said, "<u>Eating with unwashed hands</u> does not defile a person."

Matthew 15:20

God gave laws, also in Leviticus, about the correct way to prune fruit trees, Leviticus 19:23-25; and the correct way to plant seeds in a field, Leviticus 19:19. And God said a field is to be worked for six years, and on the seventh year the field is to be given a year's rest, Leviticus 25:1-7. Did Jesus do away with those laws? No! Of course not. When farmers don't obey God's agricultural laws, they produce food that's harmful to people's health. Some people say Christians are anti-science. No. Our God created the science that governs the world. He gave us scientific laws that, if followed, will bring health and prosperity. Disobeying them is foolish and sinful, and will bring disease and misery. God's science doesn't change. Eating pigs causes disease. Hunting, storing, selling, and eating bats causes disease.　　Deuteronomy 28:58-61

HOLY
BIBLE

> If you were given the whole world,
> could you enjoy it, knowing you
> had to trade your soul for it?
> Jesus, Matthew 16:26

Are you a pro athlete? When your team tells you to wear something on your uniform that promotes evil, and you know it's wrong, do you silently go along, or do you refuse to wear it?

In Matthew 4:8-10, the devil told Jesus, "Worship me and I'll give you the world." Jesus said <u>no</u> to the devil by speaking truth from the Bible, from Deuteronomy 6:13-14 and 10:20. Will you say no to the devil and speak truth from the Bible, knowing that people will hate you for it? Christians have to be willing to lose everything for Jesus.

> If you try to save your life, you'll lose it.
> But, if you lose your life for Me, you'll save it.
> Jesus, Luke 9:24

Hebrews 12:2 says Jesus was willing to endure shame and humiliation so He could take the punishment for your sins. Roman soldiers stripped Jesus naked, publicly. They whipped, punched, and spit on Jesus while people watched. Then they nailed Jesus to a cross. He hung there in unimaginable pain while people yelled insults at Him and laughed at Him, Matthew 27:27-44; John 19:1-3. Are you unwilling to be publicly shamed and humiliated for Him? Do you want the riches, fame, and glory of this temporary world, or the eternal glory of Heaven? Will you shake hands with the devil and trade your soul for the world by silently celebrating evil for your team?

> If you agree with Me, and you say the same thing that I say,
> and you do it publicly, admit in front of people that you
> love Me – by obeying Me, then, when I stand before My Father
> who is in Heaven, I will tell Him all about what you did for Me.
> But if you stay silent, if you don't speak up, and you make believe
> that you don't know Me, then, when I stand before My Father who
> is in Heaven, I will also stay silent, as though you never existed.
> Jesus, Matthew 10:32-33

MY
SOUL

> If you won't pick up your own cross and
> follow Me, then you can't be My disciple.
> Jesus, Luke 14:27

Jesus compared becoming His disciple to a most terrifying experience. They were living under the Roman government, who executed people by nailing them to a cross in a public place. People were forced to carry the cross they would die on to the place of their execution, John 19:17. Jesus lived a life of sorrow, Isaiah 53:1-12. He was hated, betrayed, and executed on false charges. Jesus told His followers that we too will be hated, John 15:18-21. Every day, in many places in the world, Christians are tortured, put into forced labor camps, raped, and killed. Their children are taken away, and they lose everything they own because they're Christians, 2 Timothy 3:12. And now, in America, the Beacon of Christianity to the world, Christians lose their jobs, and are silenced, slandered, banned, physically battered, and murdered. You don't hear about the evil done to Christians in America because the mainstream media and those in government at this time won't talk about it.

Jesus took up His cross so He could be crucified by Roman soldiers, to pay for the sins of anyone who would believe in Him. Christians don't take up our cross to pay for our sins. Taking up our cross means we're willing to die for Jesus. Jesus told the apostle Peter that he would be killed for being a Christian, John 21:18-19. The apostle James, brother of the apostle John, was killed because he was a Christian, Acts 12:1-2. God puts genuine Bible-affirming Christians through a radical transformation. He gives us the ability to do what pleases Him, and we speak the truth from the Bible, unashamed, with childlike sincerity, boldy proclaiming God's Word regardless of the consequences. And because we do that, we don't live lives of popularity and celebrity. The apostles were beaten for teaching people about Jesus. But when they were released, they rejoiced, and thanked God for counting them worthy to suffer for Jesus, Acts 5:40-42. Jesus gives genuine Christians real peace, and real joy, and eternal life.

Many of the preachers and politicians who call themselves Christians are counterfeit Christians. They're grinning ghouls, who glibly recite Bible verses, Matthew 4:6.

> Man shall not live by bread alone,
> but by every word that proceedeth
> out of the mouth of God.
> Jesus, Matthew 4:4 (KJV)

The KJV says, "man." But in the original Greek, the word is *anthropos*. It's where we get the English word anthropology, meaning the study of people. *Anthropos* means people, male and female. Jesus is saying you were not given the precious gift of human life just so you could eat bread (food) to give life to your physical body. You were given that gift so you could eat every word that comes from the mouth of God, so you can receive an eternal spiritual body. We find every word that comes from the mouth of God in the most valuable thing in the whole world, the most precious gift God has left us – the Holy Bible. Why did America become the greatest land of freedom and prosperity that has ever existed? Why did America become the nation that ended slavery? It's because the sinners who founded America acknowledged the Creator in America's founding document. They studied the Bible in the halls of government and bought Bibles to put in schools. "Blessed is the nation whose God is the Lord," Psalms 33:12 (KJV). But everything's changed. America is committing suicide. The devil and his agents removed the Bible from schools. The Bible is vilified, banned, and hated. Instead of teaching the Bible, schools teach racial hatred, sexual perversion, hatred of God's restrainers of evil – the police, hatred of the Bible and Christians, hatred of capitalism, and hatred of America. The state is taking away the authority of parents over their children. Those are all tenets of Marxism. People in Communist countries fly the American flag, and yearn for the freedom that's no longer appreciated by Americans. God is punishing Americans by taking away the ability to enjoy life that previous generations had. People don't know what life is for. America's rejection of the Bible is why there's more crime and violence, more deaths of despair from drugs and alcohol, a lower quality of life, the inability to win wars, and an economy hopelessly in debt. And it will get much worse, 2 Timothy 3:1-5, 12-13. When Jesus returns He will appear suddenly, to catch people by surprise. Jesus will destroy the devil and his followers, 2 Peter 3:10. Look up the word "quickly," # 5035, that Jesus used in Revelation 22:20 to describe His return.

It says in Luke 15:2 that Jesus ate with sinners. And Matthew 11:19 says Jesus was the friend of sinners. Actually, both of those statements were accusations made by people who hated Jesus. They didn't want anyone to follow Him. So, they implied that the reason Jesus ate with, and was the friend of sinners, was because Jesus was a sinner too.

There are people today who hate Jesus. And of course, they call themselves Christians. They say Jesus was committed to diversity and inclusion, and that He practiced radical love by welcoming the oppressed and marginalized to eat with Him. And they deceive you by being vague, never coming to a point, never explicitly stating what they mean. What they want you to think they mean is that Jesus shared His life with unrepentant sexually immoral people and never spoke a discouraging word to them. They want you to think Jesus was a sinner.

Deceivers don't tell you that Jesus divides people, Matthew 25:31-33. Jesus turned away people who didn't want to obey Him, Mark 10:17-25; Luke 9:57-62; John 2:23-25. Jesus is God the Judge, Revelation 6:15-17. Jesus hates evil, and loves good, Amos 5:15; Revelation 2:2,6. Jesus is angry with evildoers, Mark 3:5; Revelation 6:15-17. Jesus is blunt about sin. He said repent of your sin or you'll die in hell, Luke 13:1-5.

Deceivers trick you by never telling you the reason why Jesus ate with sinners. Jesus told us why. He said it was to call them to repentance, Mark 2:15-17. Jesus is the best friend a sinner can have because Jesus can save a sinner from their slavery to sin, and give them eternal life.

Jesus said there's only one way you can become His friend. He said, "You are My friends if you do what I command you," John 15:14. If you don't want to obey Jesus, you're making yourself His enemy, James 4:4. Jesus saves people who admit their sinfulness, who are crushed and brokenhearted over their sin, Isaiah 57:15; 66:2. Jesus was at the house of a man named Zacchaeus. And Zacchaeus stood up and told Jesus that he is repenting of (changing his mind about) his sins. Zacchaeus confessed his sins to Jesus, and Zacchaeus forsook his sins. And Jesus said, "Today, salvation has come to this house," Luke 19:1-10.

Yes, Jesus is inclusive. He welcomes all sinners to repent of their sin.

A woman cried out to Jesus, "Oh Lord, have mercy on me, my daughter is possessed by a demon." But Jesus ignored her. Then she asked Him again. She said, "Lord, help me." Jesus responded by saying, "It wouldn't be fair to take the children's bread, and give it to the dogs." And she replied, "That's true, Lord, but the dogs eat the crumbs that fall from their owner's table." And Jesus said, "Wow! You're a woman who possesses a tremendous amount of faith. It will be just as you wish." When Jesus said that, the woman's daughter was immediately freed from the demon, Matthew 15:21-28.

The devil will use anything to lead you away from Jesus. You might have noticed that when someone insults a religious leader, the result is angry cries of protest. But insult Jesus, and there's silence. Some clever people are using that phenomenon as camouflage to disseminate their racial hatred of white people, without reproach. They've created the perfect punching bag, in the contemptible character called White Jesus. Here's their interpretation of the encounter between Jesus and the woman: a brown woman pleaded with White Jesus to heal her daughter. But He ignored her and called her a dog because White Jesus is a racist. So, the brown woman rebuked White Jesus and taught him that racism is a sin. And White Jesus repented of his sin of racism, and healed her daughter. No. The reason Real Jesus ignored her is because God had a plan. He chose Abraham, who had a grandson named Israel. And it would be through the children of Israel that God would bring salvation to the world. So, it was "fair" then that when the the Savior, Real Jesus, arrived, that He would go to those "children" first. The woman wasn't one of them. She was a Canaanite. But she didn't say, "Heal my daughter, or I'll have you cancelled, you white supremacist." She humbled herself before Real Jesus. She knew the reason He said "dogs" (Greek, *kunarion*: puppies; not, *kuon*: evil people) was to explain the sequence of salvation. And, by the end of the conversation, she was one of the children eating at the table.

The devil makes good use of White Jesus. The devil wants you to go to hell. So, he makes you reject the Savior, Real Jesus, by making you think He was just a man, a sinner, a white supremacist, White Jesus. Then the devil leads you to Marxist Jesus.

In a Communist country, the state is god. So, Christianity is banned. One country is trying to pacify its people. They let them have Bibles, but they force them to only use Bibles that are published by the government. That government knows the message of the Bible, and, they've destroyed it. Their Bibles teach that Jesus sinned.

The message of the Bible, from beginning to end, is about sin. All of us inherited a sinful heart from the first man, Adam, Romans 5:12. We sin when we break God's laws, 1 John 3:4. We find His laws in the Bible, and in nature, Romans 1:18-20. Everyone sins, Romans 3:23. Everyone dies because of sin, 1 Corinthians 15:21-22. Christian's physical bodies can get sick and die prematurely because of sin, 1 Corinthians 11:29-30. And, because of sin, souls die in hell, Romans 6:23 (but not Christian's).

God is merciful. He loves people, 1 John 4:8,10,16. So, He came up with the principle of substitution. In the Old Testament, God told the people of Israel that instead of them dying for their sin, they could kill lambs and other animals as a substitute, Leviticus 17:11. But that only kept them from being punished with death. It didn't change their sinful heart, and it didn't save their souls from hell, Hebrews 10:4-14. God told Israel they must not sacrifice their less valuable animals. He would only accept their best animals. They had to be spotless, and without blemishes, Exodus 12:5; Leviticus 22:17-25. Killing animals for sin was meant to teach them, and us, about the One who <u>can</u> save our soul from hell, Isaiah 53:4-5; 1 Peter 2:24; Revelation 1:5.

One day, John the Baptist saw Jesus, and he said to two of his disciples, "Look! there's the Lamb of God, who takes away the sin of the world," John 1:29,36. Jesus is the One. Those who believe in His death and resurrection, live forever, John 11:20-27. If Jesus sinned, then all of Christianity collapses. If Jesus sinned, then He couldn't be the spotless, sinless sacrifice for sin, He couldn't save anyone. And Jesus Himself would be punished for His sin by being killed in hell. But, Jesus is sinless, 2 Corinthians 5:21; 1 Peter 1:18-19; Hebrews 4:15. Jesus is God, John 1:1-4,14,18; Colossians 2:9; Titus 2:13-14; Revelation 1:17-18.

There is no sin in Jesus.
1 John 3:5

It won't go well for you if you try to hide your sins from God.
But if you weep and wail from sadness over your sins, and you
declare war on your sins, then God will show you mercy.
Proverbs 28:13

You can't hide your sins from God,

The eyes of the Lord see everything.
He observes good people and evil people.
Proverbs 15:3

Numbers 32:23 says you can be sure that your sin will find you. It
means sin has consequences. David prayed this to God,

I kept silent about my sins. But I was dying.
I groaned day and night from the weight of Your hand on me.
Life lost its sweetness. I was walking through a desert. Selah

But then I stopped trying to hide my sins from You.
I said, "I will confess my sins to the Lord."
So, I told You about the evil things I did.
And You forgave me. You freed me from the guilt. Selah
That's why everyone who loves holiness,
prays to You in this season of mercy.
Psalms 32:3-6

The word Selah means – stop and think about what was just said.

When you stop trying to fool God, you'll be blissful,
because God will put the punishment for your sins on Jesus,
and He will clothe you in the pure holiness of Jesus.
When God takes the guilt off your back and throws it away
because you trust in the sacrificial death of the Lord Jesus,
then you'll experience true joy, happiness and contentment.
Psalms 32:1-2

(Continued on page 112)

MY
SINS

Are you wondering why I say some things over and over? It's because repetition is a good teacher. That's why God uses it in the Bible.

And I repeat things because Christians need to be constantly reminded of what God had to do to save us from sin, so we don't forget how serious sin is. The Bible teaches us over and over, from beginning to end, about the seriousness of sin. You could say the Bible is about sin. So, we need to hear about it over and over.

If you knew that Jesus was returning tonight, what would you do? Would you look at people with lust? Would you fantasize about how you'd like to get back at someone who did you wrong? Or would you be on your knees crying out to God? And would you dust off your Bible and read it? God wants you to do those things now, today, and every day. The Bible tells us to stop sinning, to live holy lives, and be perfect. Jesus said, "Be perfect, like God is perfect," Matthew 5:48. Christians are striving for perfection.

If you're a fellow Christian, then think about this,

> I was crucified (died) with Christ. But I live.
> Though it's not me. It's Christ living in me.
> Paul, Galatians 2:20

John 14:23 says Jesus makes His home in a Christian's heart – actually. Are you a Christian? Do you want to be successful in resisting sin? Then the next time you want to look at porn, or smoke weed, or be unkind to someone, or commit any other sin, remind yourself that Jesus is living in your heart. And ask yourself if you want to do that sin with Jesus right there with you. Would you do it if Jesus was sitting in the room with you? But He is in the room with you.

When you remember that, you'll get back in your right mind and walk away from that sin. I hate the idea of sinning with Jesus living in my heart. It gives me a strong desire to resist sin, and the ability to avoid it. When God gives you His Holy Spirit, and you know for sure that God exists, and you understand what He said in the Bible, then you'll have an intense desire to keep yourself from sin.

There's a lot of beauty in this world, and a lot of pleasures. Why? Because God is merciful. He freely gives everyone some of the good things that were in the world when He created it perfect, Matthew 5:45. But, because of sin, this world is a nightmare. How so? All of us end up in a coffin. And not after a trillion years, but in less than 130 years. Is that a long time? It takes God longer than that to blink His eyes.

And what good would a trillion years be if you still end up in a coffin? Only forever will do. People go through life like they have all the time in the world. They pacify themselves by planning for their retirement. Really? That's your Heaven?

Today is the day to get right with God. Yes, I'm thinking of you, my old friend. It's time to give up the booze. And you're wrong, you don't have an arrangement with God that makes it okay, as you claim. God said in the Bible that He doesn't want you in Heaven if you refuse to deal with it, 1 Corinthians 6:9-11. You say you're a Christian, but the evidence says otherwise. The fact that you think God is okay with it shows that something's very wrong. A Christian can't continue in uninterrupted, unabated, unrepented alcoholism, year after year, as you've been doing. There should be a struggle, not surrender.

No, I can't twist your arm. And I can't say, "What about the four beers?" But I can give you the truth from the Bible. It's between you and God. Yes, it will be painful. But you'll do it when you're convinced. You'll change your mind when God touches your heart. Ask him to. Today. Then, study the Bible, sincerely, and ask God what He wants you to do. If you do decide to stop drinking, it will have to be done under your doctor's supervision. Godspeed and fare-thee-well. That means I wish you success in your new endeavor, and that you do it to to perfection.

What you see in that drawing is the worst thing that can happen to a person. Will it make you change your mind about rejecting Jesus?

Jesus told a story about ten bridesmaids. They were waiting for the door to open so they could go in to the wedding. Five of them were obedient. They brought extra oil so they could keep their lamps burning while they waited.

The other five were worthless. They didn't bring extra oil. So, they ran out of oil, and had to go buy some. While they were away buying the oil, the Bridegroom arrived. And the five obedient bridesmaids went with Him into the wedding. But when the five worthless bridesmaids came back from buying the oil, they were too late, the door was closed, and they were shut out – forever.   Matthew 25:1-13

The Bridegroom is Jesus. The wedding is when Jesus returns to take all the Christians to be with Him forever in Heaven, 2 Corinthians 11:2; Ephesians 5:25-27,32; Revelation 19:7-9. The ten bridesmaids are all those who call themselves Christians. The five worthless bridesmaids might have been Bible teachers, or might have done many wonderful good deeds – but it was all an act. They looked like they were obeying Jesus. But they weren't really obeying Him, Matthew 7:21-23. They didn't love Jesus, John 14:24.

Jesus is making the point that if you say you're a Christian, then you better be sure you really are one. A lot of people taste Christianity, but they never fully partake. They have some light, but not enough. They look, act, and talk like Christians, but they're counterfeits. Churches are overrun with them.   Matthew 13:36-43;
Hebrews 6:4-6; 10:28-29

When the five worthless bridesmaids returned from buying oil, and found the door to the wedding closed, they said, "Lord, Lord, open the door, and let us in." And Jesus said to them, "Truly, I don't know you." If you're an unbeliever, then seeing what happened to those five worthless bridesmaids should make you fall to the floor and cry out to God to save you.

CLOSED

> Some people know what it takes to get to Heaven.
> They're like the pearl merchant, who found a pearl of
> incomparable rarity. And he sold every pearl he had to
> get the money to buy that one pearl.
>> Jesus, Matthew 13:45-46

No, Jesus is not saying you can buy your way into Heaven. God is love, 1 John 4:8,16. God gave us all of His love when He put aside everything He had so He could be executed for us, Philippians 2:5-8. God wants you in Heaven if you appreciate that, and if you're willing to love like that. Jesus wants all of your love, all of your heart, mind, soul, and strength, Mark 12:30. God wants you in Heaven if you understand that salvation is a free gift – but it costs you everything. That doesn't mean you send away your loved ones and give away all your possessions. Stay with your spouse and love them. Enjoy the gift of marriage God gave you. The man in the drawing represents someone who is willing to risk losing everything he has for Jesus. It's a state of mind. Jesus said you can't be His disciple if you're not willing to risk losing everything you have for Him, Luke 14:25-33.

A lot of people passed by the pearl in the window. Maybe they glanced at it, but they didn't buy it. Most people don't love God enough to be willing to give up their sin. They love their sin. They love money and the pleasures of this world more than they love God, 1 John 2:15-17. And most people want to avoid the pain, humiliation, and loss that comes with the pearl, with being a follower of Jesus.

> We have to go through a lot of suffering
> on the road that leads to Heaven.
>> Acts 14:22

> Everyone will hate you because you follow Me.
>> Jesus, Mark 13:13

But the people who avoid the pearl don't know that those of us who bought the pearl, count it all joy to suffer for Jesus.
>> Matthew 5:10-12; John 15:18-21; Acts 5:40-42; 16:16-25
>> 2 Timothy 2:3; 3:12; James 1:2-4; 1 Peter 4:12-14

Pearl
of
Great Price

> Come to Me, all of you who are overloaded
> and fatigued from toil. I will refresh you.
> Take My yoke upon you, and learn about Me.
> I am gentle and lowly in heart.
> You'll find rest for your soul, because
> My yoke is easy, and My baggage is light.
> Jesus, Matthew 11:28-30

If you're going to use two animals to pull a wagon, you hold them together with a piece of wood called a yoke.

Read carefully what Jesus said. There are three things you have to do. Jesus said, "Come to Me." You have to choose to act and go to Him. Then Jesus said, "Take My yoke upon you." You have to take the yoke from Him, and put it on. And Jesus said, "Learn about me." The Bible is the only place where you can learn about Jesus.

If you do those three things, then Jesus will give you rest. That means you will no longer be worn out and overburdened from trying to buy a ticket to Heaven with your own merits. Jesus has you covered. Jesus will dress you in His perfect goodness. You'll go to Heaven on His ticket. You'll never have to worry about going to Heaven. You'll be let into Heaven because you're a friend of Jesus.

How do you become His friend? Jesus said, "You're My friend if you do the things I command you," John 15:14. You're His friend if you follow His instructions, obey His laws. That's how He knows who loves Him. Those who love Him, obey Him, John 14:21. Those who don't love Him, don't obey Him, John 14:24. Jesus only wants people in Heaven who love Him. Christians don't earn our salvation by obeying Jesus. We obey Him because He loves us, and saved us, and because He gives us the ability to obey Him. Christians have a lot of hard work to do. We endure persecution from a hostile world because we speak the truth. And we have to watch out for the fiery arrows of temptations to sin that are fired at us by the devil. But the weight of those things is easy and light because we're yoked to Jesus. He is there to comfort us, fill us with joy, and help us to keep on doing the work He has for us.

> When you see fruit sprouting from a Christian,
> you're seeing the beauty of God.
> Jesus, John 15:8

Jesus is talking about spiritual fruit.

How do you grow the fruit that you eat? You sow seeds. Jesus said it's the same way with growing spiritual fruit, Matthew 13:18-23. The seeds only grow in the right soil. Jesus said He is the Sower. The seed He sows is the Word of God, the Bible. Jesus said some hearts won't receive the seed because they're too hard. Some hearts do receive the seed but can't grow much fruit because they fear persecution, or they love the pleasures of the world too much.

Jesus said some hearts are prepared to receive the seed of the Bible. They want to understand and obey God's Word. They'll grow much fruit. Jesus said He is the real vine, and His disciples are His branches, and God is the Vinedresser, John 15:1-8. It means God cleanses filth from true disciples so we can produce more fruit. Jesus washes us with the Word of God, Ephesians 5:25-27.

If a branch doesn't produce fruit, it means they weren't a true disciple. They were an impostor. They're like a dead branch on a tree. God cuts it off, casts it aside, and it dries up. Then, the only thing it's good for is to be burned in the fire. Jesus said the fruit is the proof that someone is His true disciple. If there's no fruit sprouting from you, then you're not a Christian, you're fooling yourself.

Jesus said His disciples can't produce fruit from ourselves, just like a branch can't produce fruit if it's not attached to the vine. We can't do anything on our own. Jesus said we must stay with Him, and His words must live in us, and we must follow in His footsteps. That's when we produce much fruit, and show what God has done with us, and prove that we are His genuine disciples. We have the Bible living in our heart at all times, with our minds active, thinking, planning, praying, John 8:31. Then we become useful. We sow seeds like Jesus does, by teaching the Bible. And God gets all the glory when people come to salvation from hearing us teach them a lesson from the Bible.

> You don't know when I'll return. So, watch.
> Jesus, Matthew 25:13

The word "watch" is the Greek word *gregoreuo* (# 1127 in the Strong's). It means to snap out of it, wake up, pay attention, be on your guard, keep your eyes and ears open, know what's going on, and take all the necessary precautions. It means to stay awake, and go without sleep. Jesus is telling believers to be vigilant, eagle-eyed, with our mind fixed on Him, while we wait for Him to return, Luke 12:40.

But you've got a lot of important things you need to do right now, so you're not watching for Jesus. You'll square things up with God later on, at a more convenient time. Jesus knows what you're thinking. That's why the date of His return is a secret, Mark 13:32-37.

Jesus wants you to prepare for your death now, right now, starting today, and then every day, for the rest of your life. Then you'll be waiting for Jesus to return, like the girl in the drawing. You and her will sing the words of Psalms 130:6: "I wait for the Lord, more eagerly than a night watchman yearns for the morning to arrive."

> I will look to the Lord. I will wait for the God
> of my salvation. And my God will hear me.
> Micah 7:7

When Jesus returns, He will give all the blessings of salvation to those who looked for Him. Jesus will give the crown of righteousness to everyone who loves His return, 2 Timothy 4:8; Hebrews 9:28. If you're putting off giving your life to Jesus, then hidden deep inside you is dread, a fear of the terrible judgment you'll face when Jesus returns. Instead of staying awake, eagerly watching for Jesus, you're losing sleep watching for the fleeting pleasures and attachments of this world. If you're not watching for Jesus, you're watching for sin.

> All those who watch for sin will be destroyed.
> Isaiah 29:20

HOLY
BIBLE

Our friend Lazarus is sleeping.
Walk with Me to his house.
I'm going to wake him up.
Jesus, John 11:11

Jesus said Lazarus was sleeping. His disciples thought He meant Lazarus was actually sleeping. So, Jesus put it in words they could understand. He said, "Lazarus is dead," John 11:14. When a Christian dies, we're just sleeping, and Jesus walks to our house to wake us up. Why? Because we're His friend, John 15:14. Jesus doesn't do that for people who didn't want to be His friend. They never wake up.

I am the resurrection and the life.
Whoever believes in Me, though they die – they will live.
Whoever lives and believes in Me – they will never die.
Jesus, John 11:25-26

Christians no longer fear death. Why? Because of what Jesus did for us. It says in Hebrews 2:14-15 that God didn't put us here in these flesh bodies and then just leave us on our own. He took on a flesh body too, just like ours. And like us, He experienced death. Jesus took away the power of death from those who love Him by giving His life for us. Death, sin, and the devil have no claim on us. We're with Jesus.

Don't feel sadness and worries over our fellow Christians
who have fallen asleep. We're not like those who have no hope.
We know that Jesus died for us, and that He rose from death,
and that God brings sleeping Christians back to life with Jesus.
1 Thessalonians 4:13-14

You'll take off your body that dies, and you'll put on a body that will never die. Then you'll fully realize the prophecy in Isaiah 25:8, which says, "God will have the victory when He destroys death." And you'll understand completely these words from Hosea 13:14, "Oh death, where is your sting? Oh grave, where is your victory?"
1 Corinthians 15:54-55

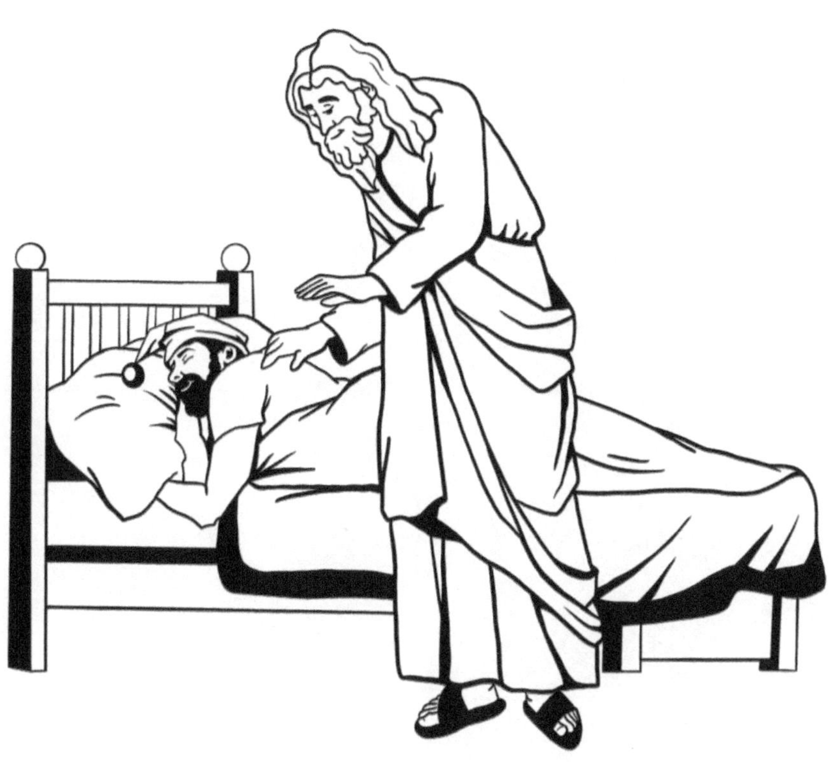

* 9 7 9 8 9 8 6 7 4 1 0 0 0 *